AF473807

MUNGO THOMSON

CRICKETS

COMPOSED BY MICHAEL WEBSTER

Other titles in this series:

Emmanuelle Antille, *Tornadoes of My Heart*
Helen Mirra, *Cloud, the, 3*
Jonathan Meese & Slavoj Zizek, *Ernteschach dem Dämon*
Peter Piller, *Teilzeitkraft*
Mungo Thomson, *Negative Space*
Stuart Bailey & Ryan Gander, *Appendix Appendix*
Peter Piller, *Nijverdal/Hellendoorn*
Matias Faldbakken, *Not Made Visible*
Johannes Wohnseifer, *Werkverzeichnis, 1992–2007*
Archiv Peter Piller, *nimmt Schaden*
Mai-Thu Perret, *Land of Crystal*
Julien Berthier, *Nothing Special*
Archiv Peter Piller, *Zeitung*
Michael Stevenson, *Celebration at Persepolis*
Jonathan Monk, *Complete Ilford Works*
Zilla Leutenegger, *Zilla and the 7th Room*
Aglaia Konrad, *Desert Cities*
Jeanne Faust, *Outlandos*
Loris Gréaud, *Cellar Door*
Claudia & Julia Müller, *Habitus vs. Habitat: Primaten*
Boris Groys & Andro Wekua, *Wait to Wait*
Korpys/Löffler, *Die Sehnsucht nach Glück...*
Anna Lea Hucht, *Sprich mit Deiner Seele*
Jonathan Monk, *Studio Visit*
Yann Sérandour, *Inside the White Cube, Overprinted Edition*
Falke Pisano, *Figures of Speech*
Heidi Specker & Theo Deutinger, *Help Me, I'm Blind*
Philip Lachenmann, *Some Scenic Views*
Ryan Gander, *Catalogue Raisonnable Vol. 1*
Hinrich Sachs, *Lost Once More*
Stefan Marx, *I guess I shouldn't be telling you*
Rita McBride, *Westways*
Mischa Kuball / Harald Welzer, *New Pott × Neue Heimat im Revier*
Gitte Villesen, *The story is not all mine, nor told by me alone*
Jakob Kolding, *Shifting Realities*
Slavs and Tatars, *Molla Nasreddin*
Archiv Peter Piller, *Kraft*

MUNGO THOMSON

CRICKETS

COMPOSED BY MICHAEL WEBSTER

Christoph Keller Editions

LA><ART

Crickets

Mungo Thomson

Composed by Michael Webster

Based upon the Frémeaux & Associés recordings *Cigales & Grillons*
by Jean C. Roché and Jean Thévenet, reference FA663
Used by permission of Frémeaux & Associés, Jean C. Roché and Jean Thévenet

This publication is part of the artists' books series
Christoph Keller Editions
Published by JRP|Ringier

LA><ART
2640 South La Cienega Boulevard, Los Angeles, California 90034
www.laxart.org

Edited by Christoph Keller
Designed by Richard Massey
Typeset in Lexicon
Printed by the Avery Group
at Shapco Printing, Inc., Minneapolis

Printed in U.S.A.

Parts are available for rental. Visit mungothomson.com for information.

ISBN 978-3-03764-334-1

Instrumentation

2 Flutes
doubling Piccolo and Pennywhistle

E-flat Clarinet

Percussion 1:
afuche
bicycle chainring
cowbell
cricket rasp
cymbal
floor tom
maraca
orchestra bells
woodblock

Percussion 2:
afuche
cowbell
cricket rasp
cricket rattle
gecko clacker
L. P. cricket
maraca
orchestra bells
shekere
Thai woodblocks

Violins
6 sections of 2 or more

duration: ca. 18 minutes

Program

Crickets

for Ensemble

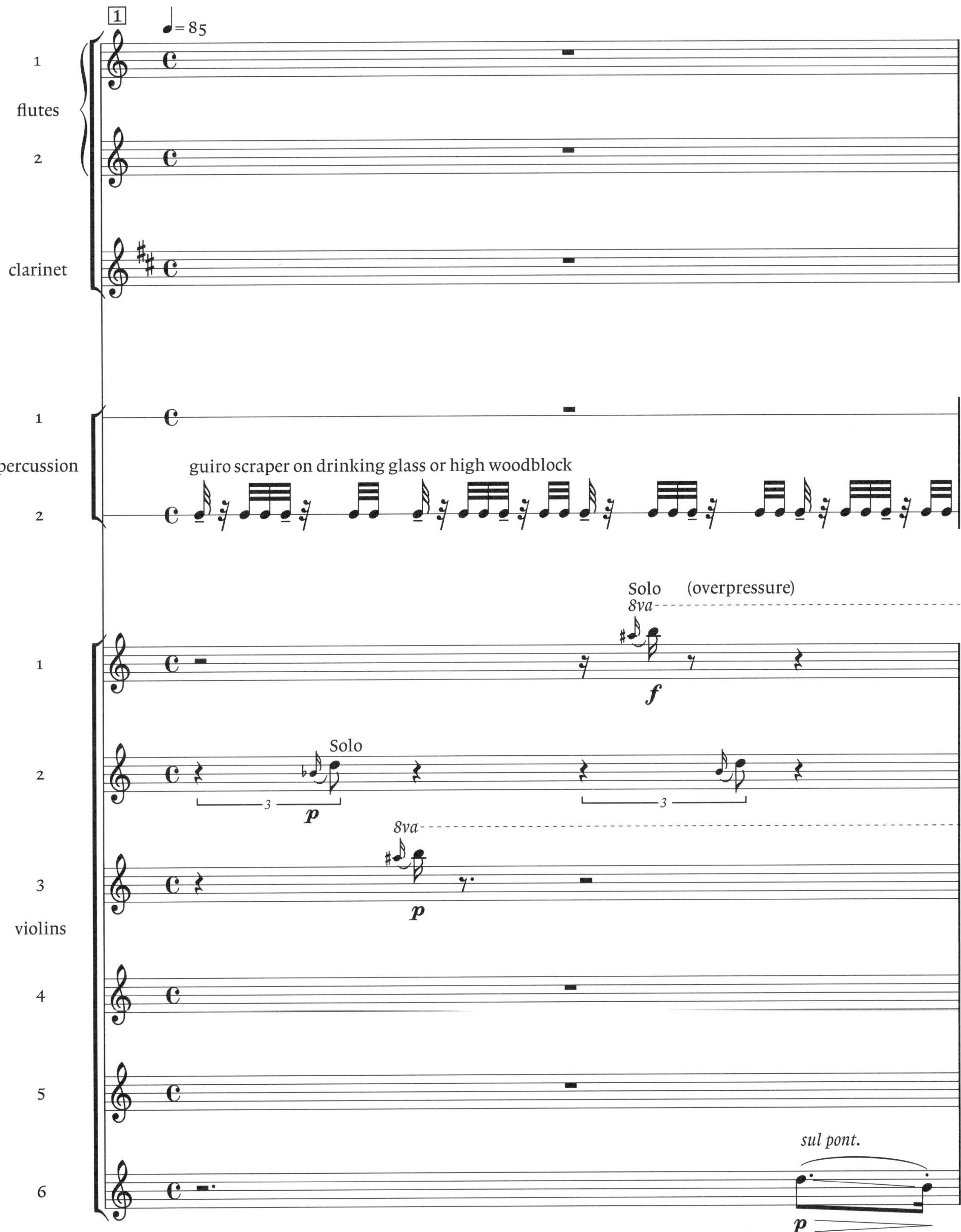

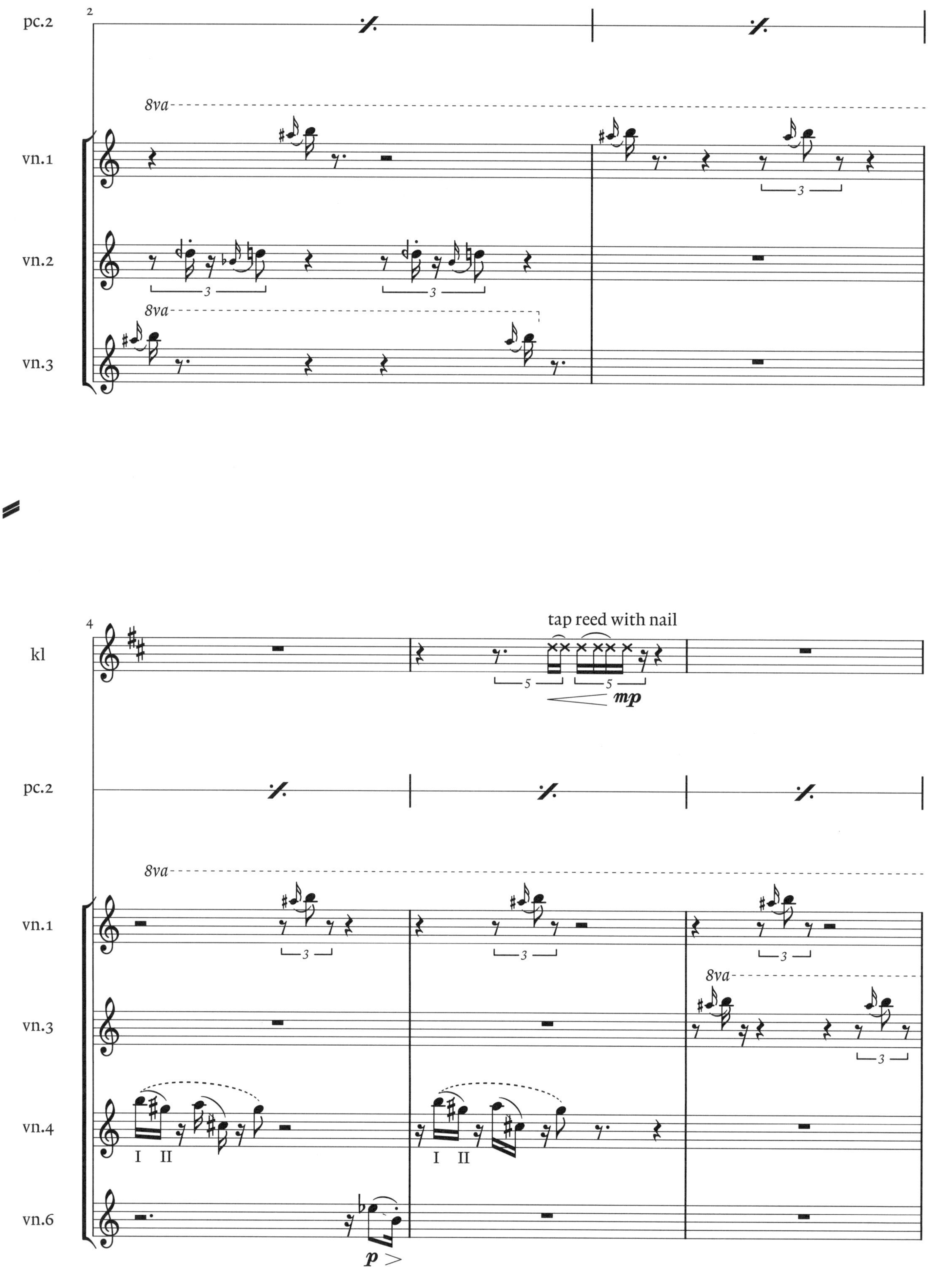

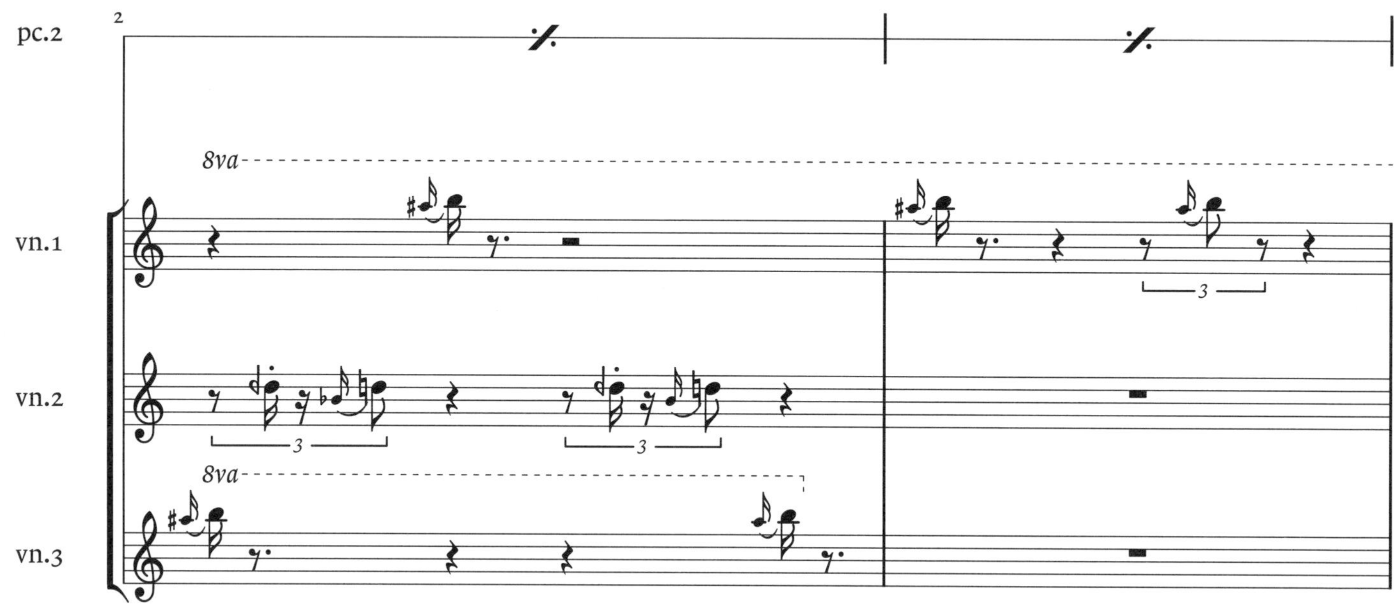

4
kl
tap reed with nail
5
5
mp
pc.2
8va
vn.1
3
3
3
vn.3
8va
3
vn.4
I II
I II
vn.6
p

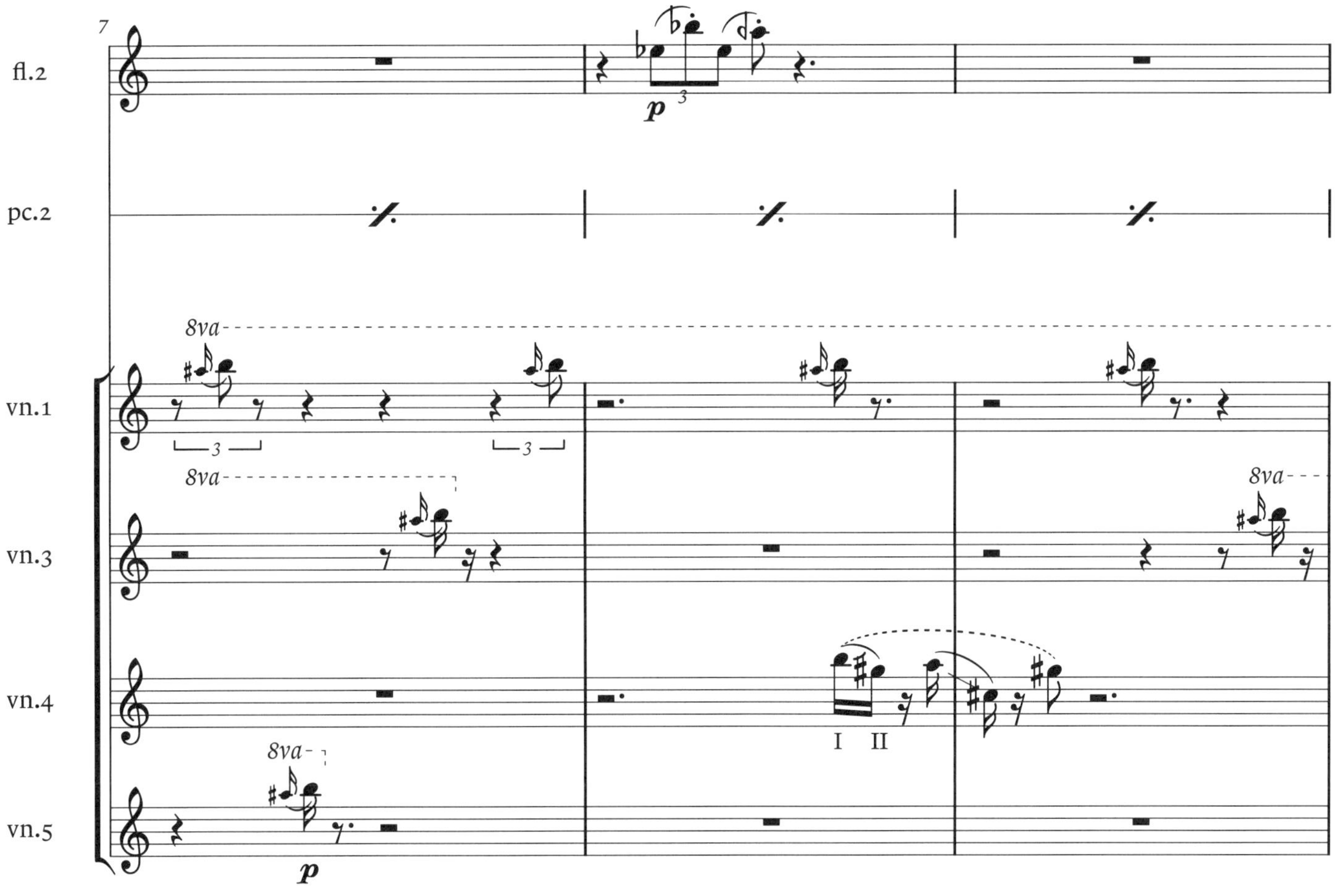
7
fl.2
pc.2
vn.1
vn.3
vn.4
vn.5
8va
p
I II

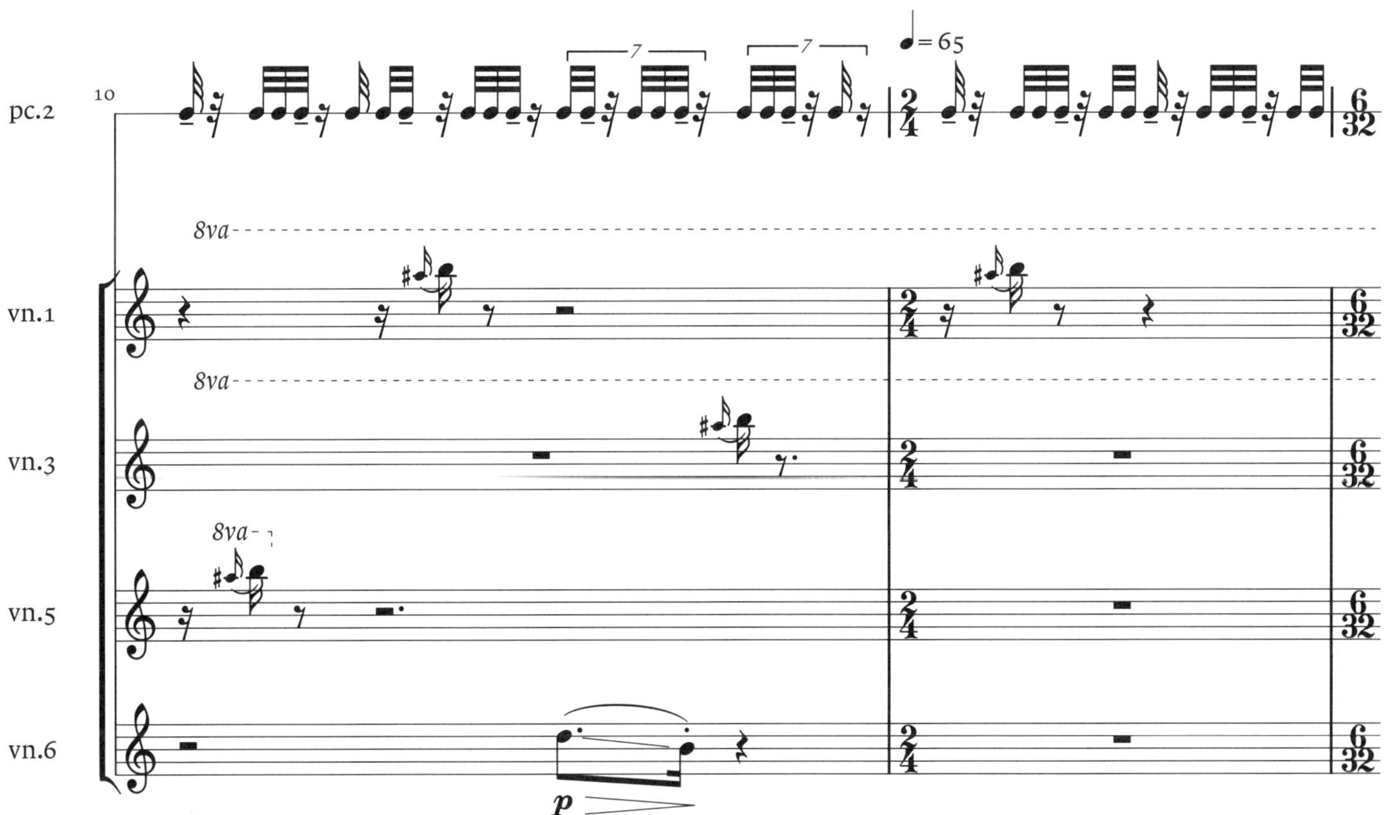
10
pc.2
vn.1
vn.3
vn.5
vn.6
8va
♩= 65
p

12

♩= 85

fl.1

mf

kl

3

p

pc.2

8va

vn.1

8va

vn.3

8va

vn.5

3

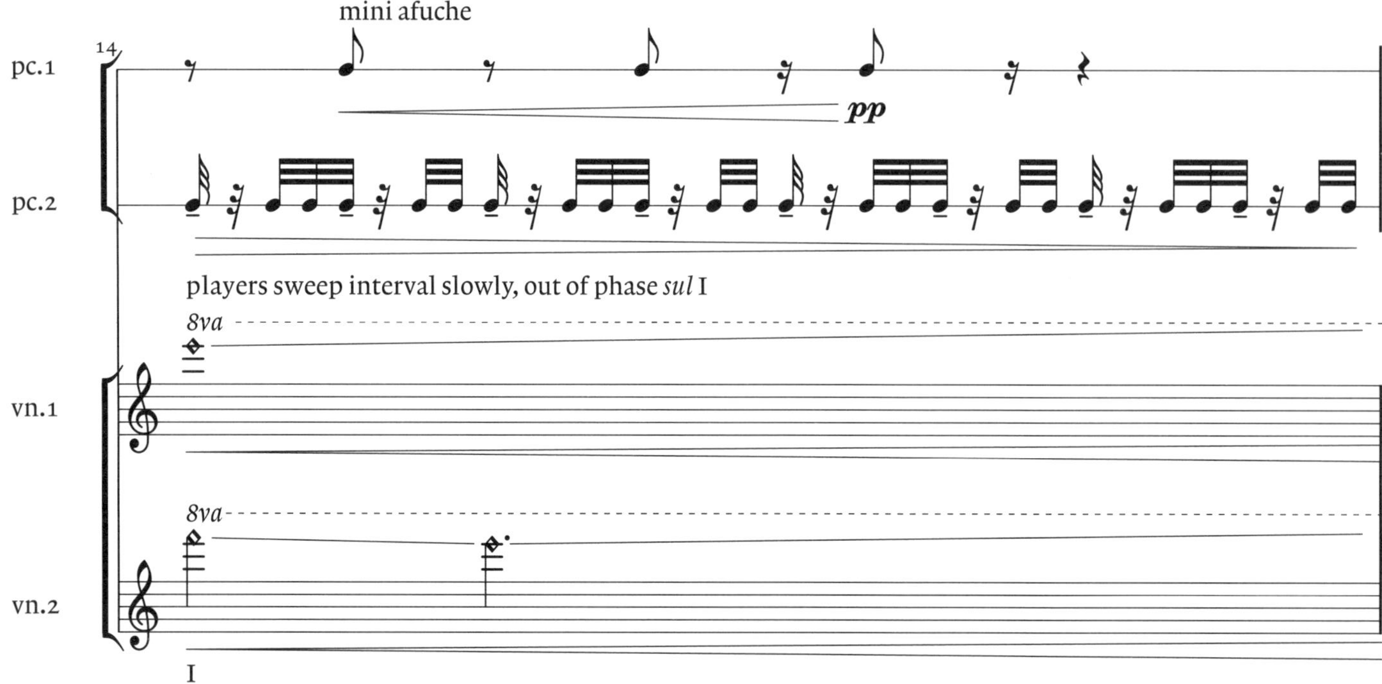

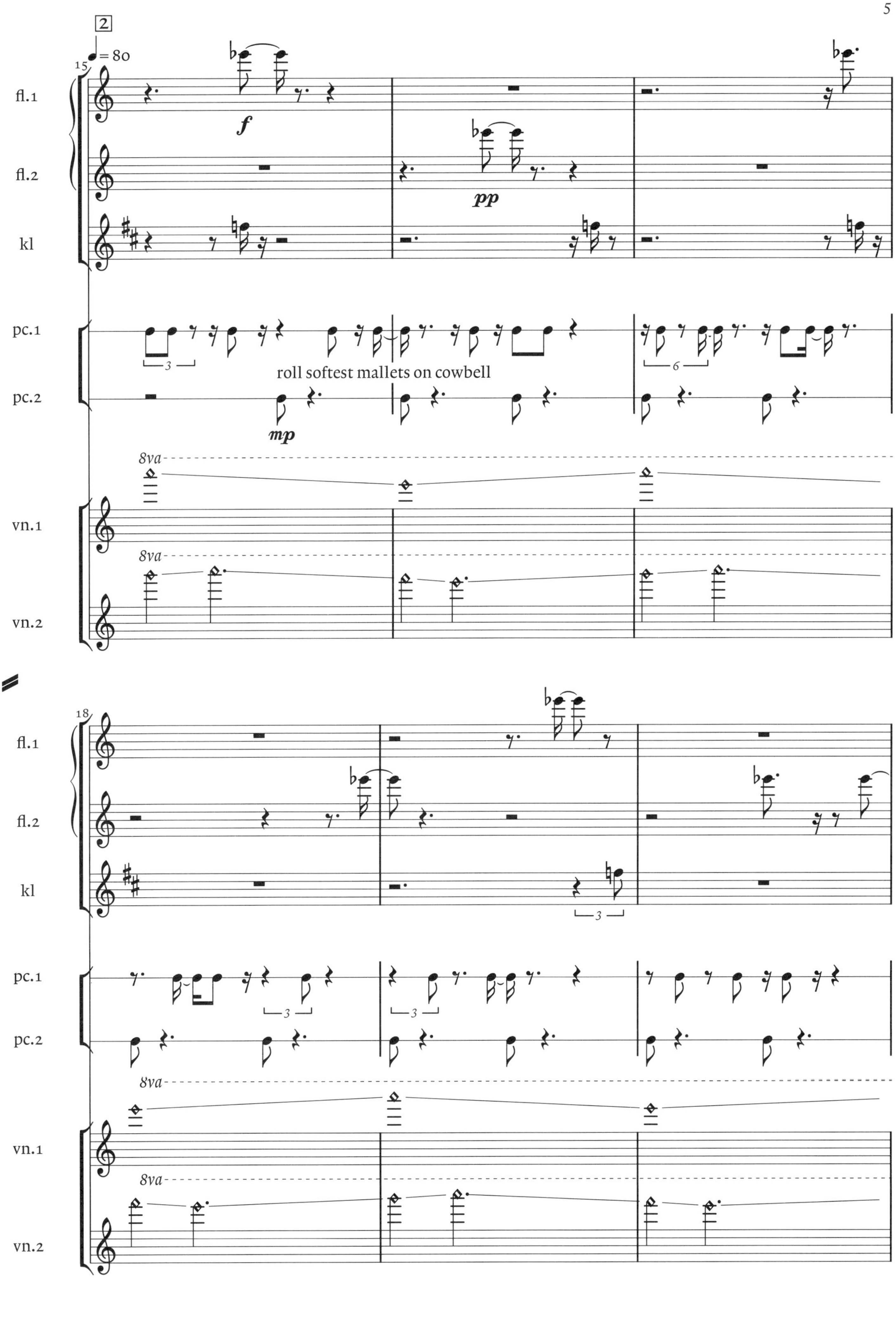

2
♩= 80
15
fl.1
fl.2
kl
f
pp
pc.1
pc.2
3
6
roll softest mallets on cowbell
mp
8va
vn.1
vn.2
18
3

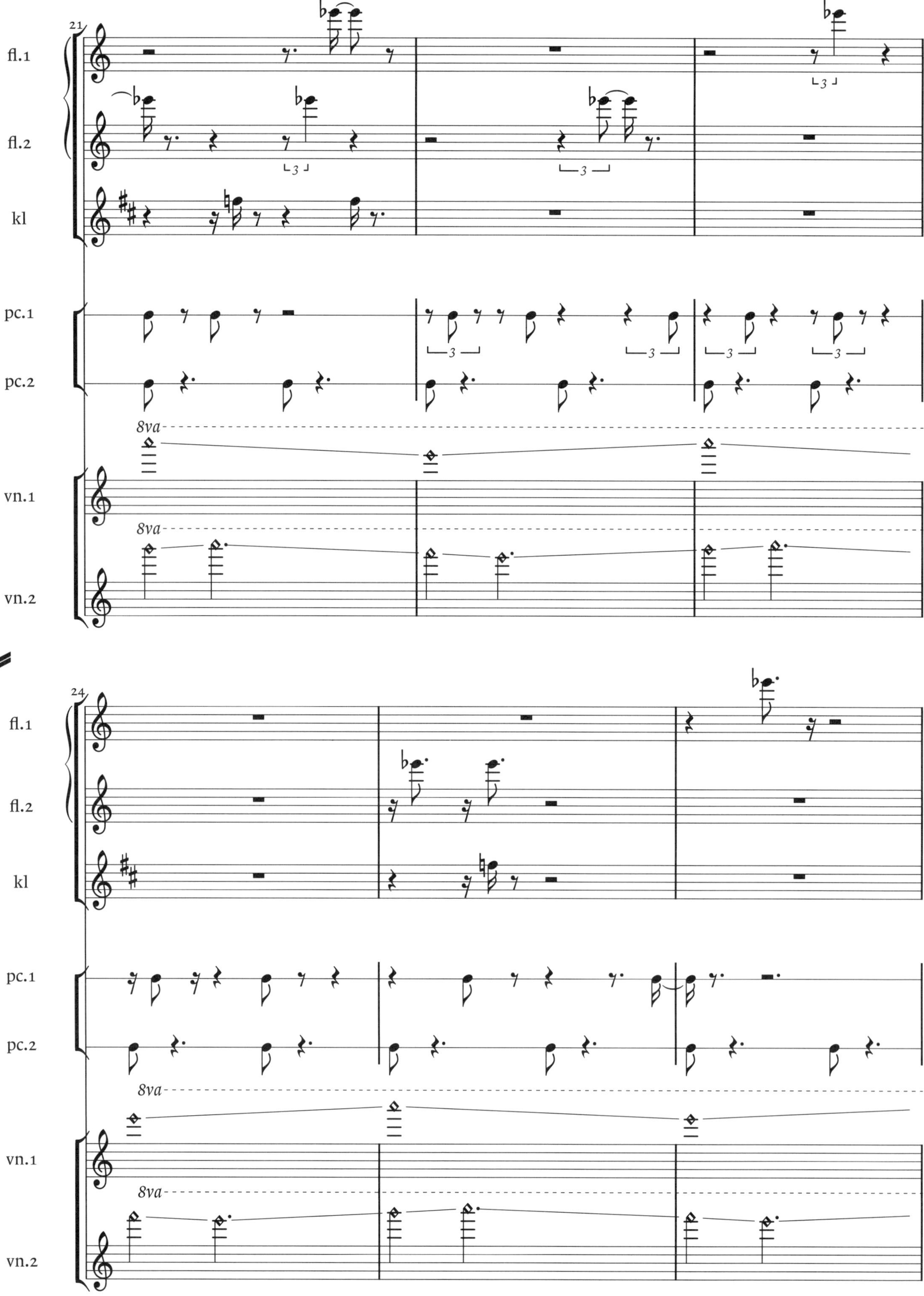
21
fl.1
fl.2
kl
pc.1
pc.2
8va
vn.1
8va
vn.2
24
fl.1
fl.2
kl
pc.1
pc.2
8va
vn.1
8va
vn.2

27
3
♩= 145
fl.1
fl.2
piccolo
flutter
f
pc.1
rasp muted cowbell with rhythm-stick (lower)
mp
3
pc.2
rasp muted cowbell with rhythm-stick (higher)
mp
vn.1
8va
mp
vn.2
8va
mp
vn.3
p
vn.4
p
vn.5
15ma
mf
vn.6
15ma
f

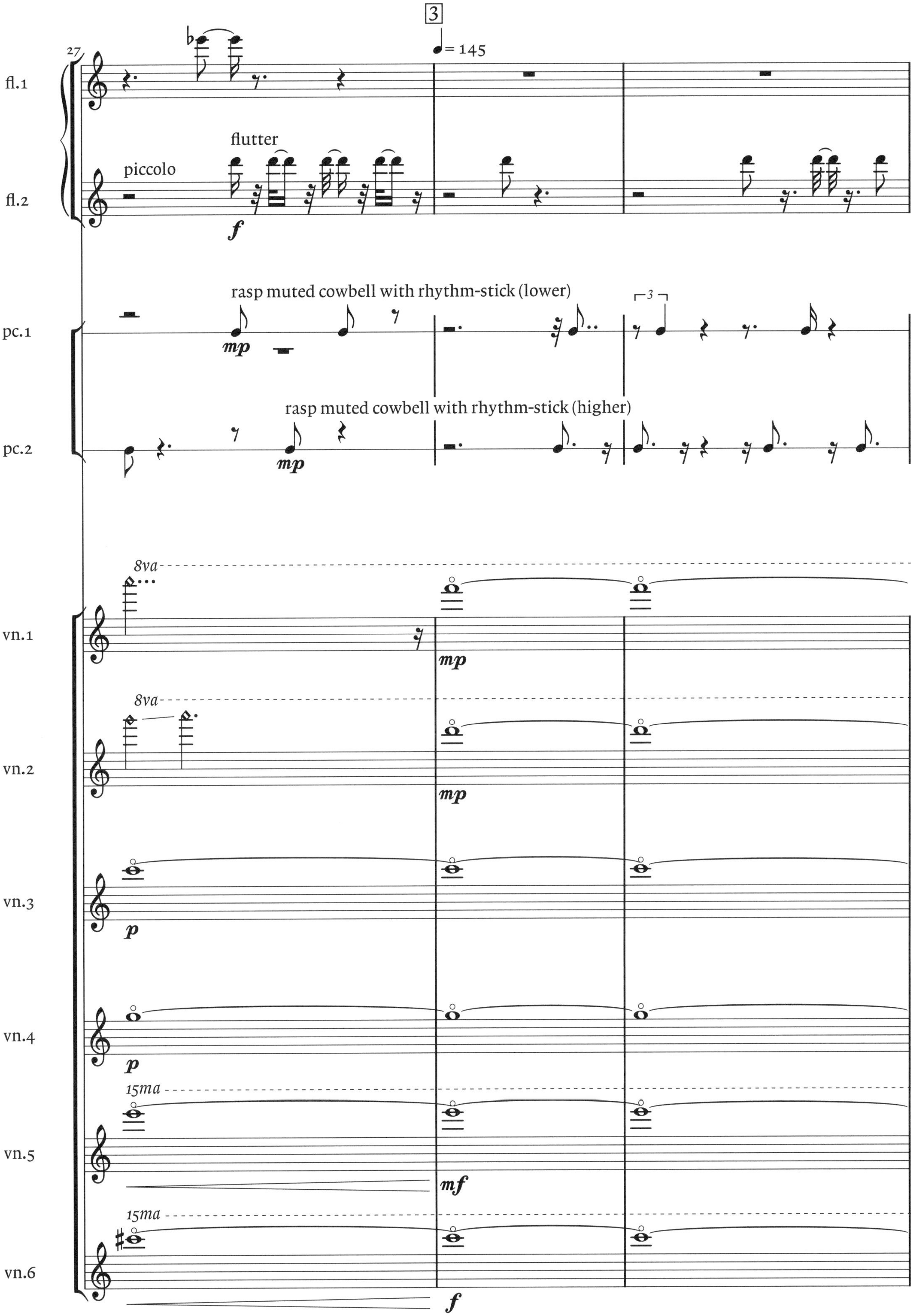

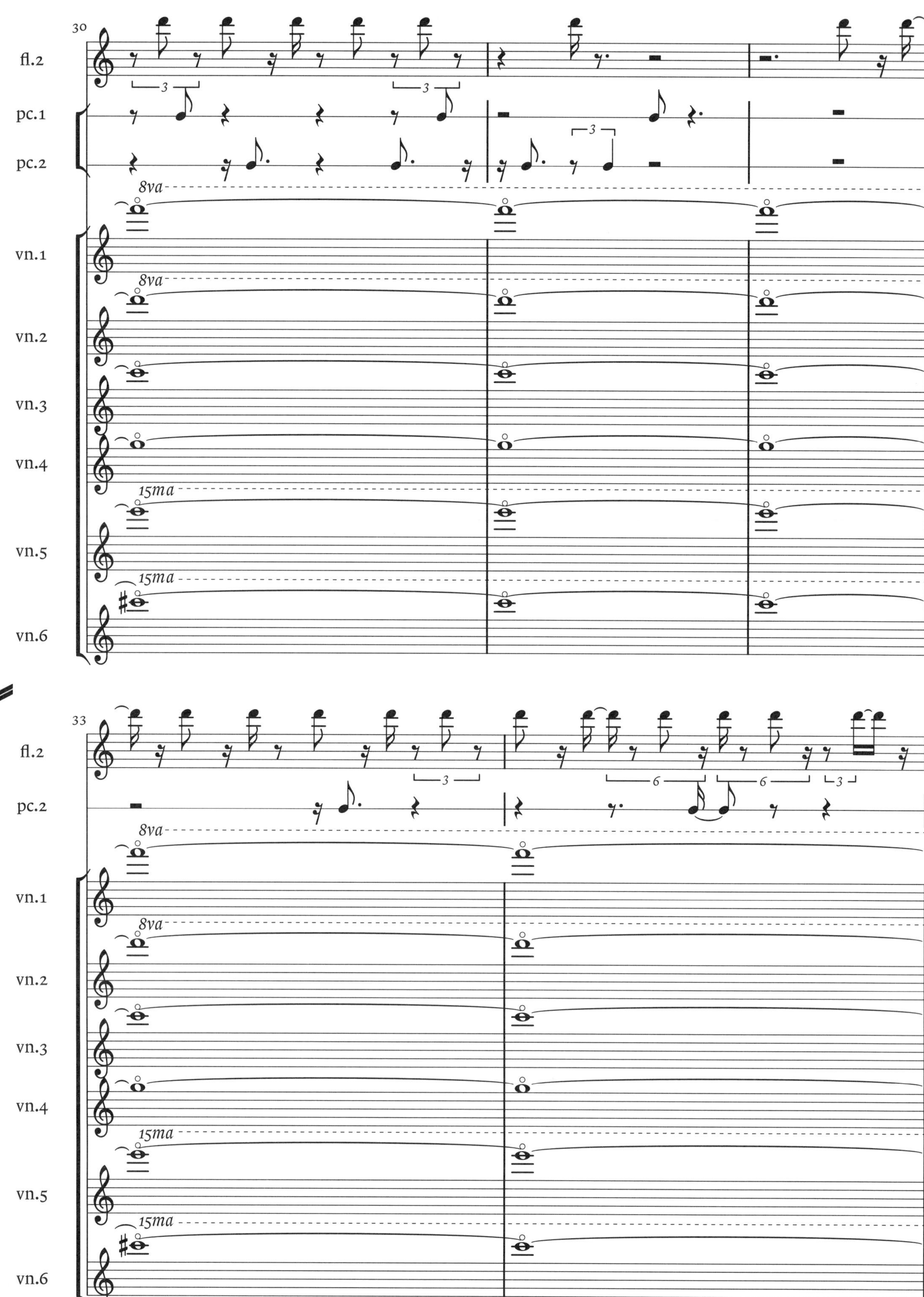
30
fl.2
pc.1
pc.2
8va
vn.1
8va
vn.2
vn.3
vn.4
15ma
vn.5
15ma
vn.6
33
fl.2
pc.2
8va
vn.1
8va
vn.2
vn.3
vn.4
15ma
vn.5
15ma
vn.6

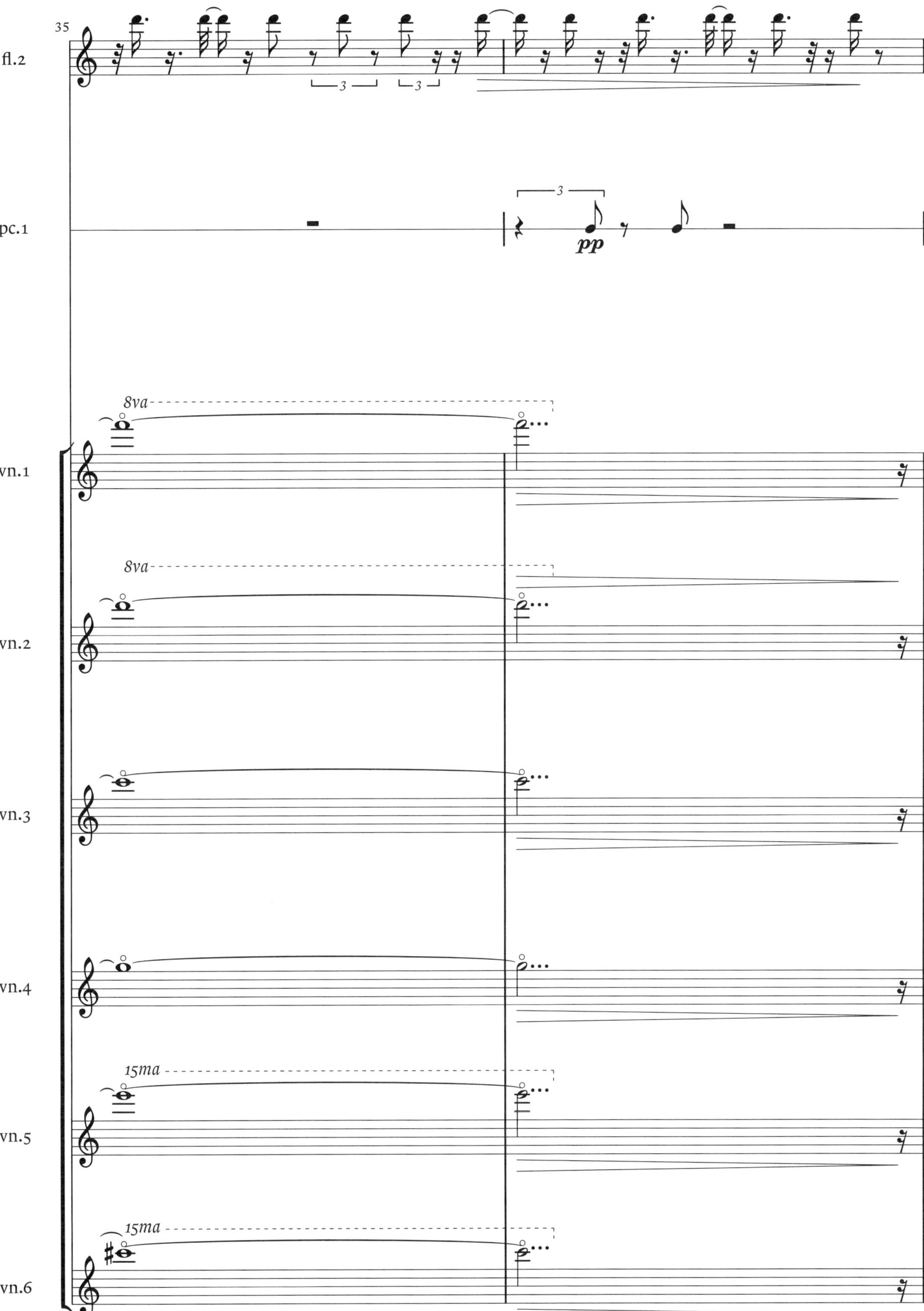
35
fl.2
3
3
pc.1
3
pp
8va
vn.1
8va
vn.2
vn.3
vn.4
15ma
vn.5
15ma
vn.6

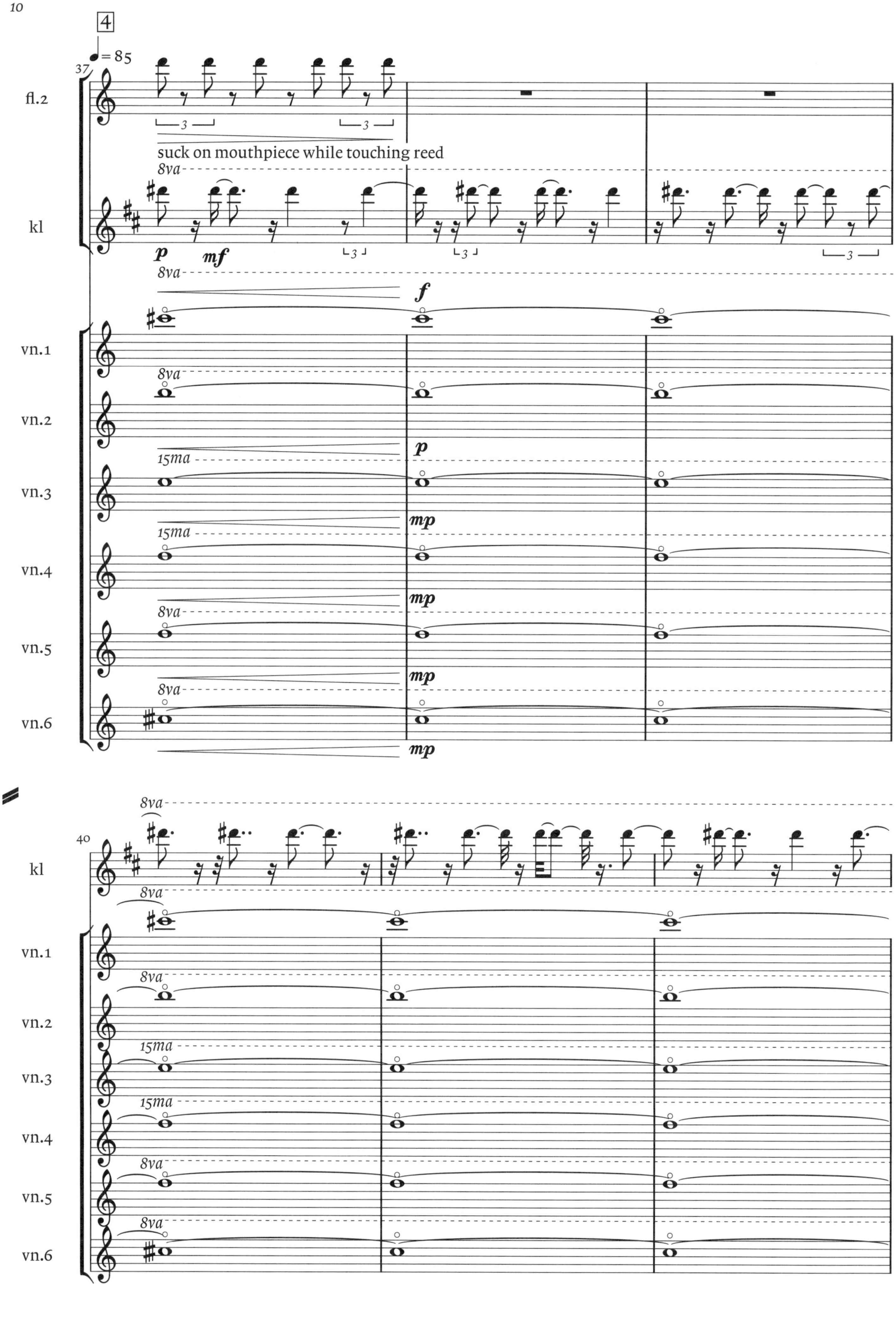

4

♩= 85

37

fl.2

suck on mouthpiece while touching reed

kl

p *mf*

8va

f

vn.1

vn.2

p

15ma

vn.3

mp

vn.4

mp

vn.5

mp

vn.6

mp

40

kl

vn.1

vn.2

vn.3

vn.4

vn.5

vn.6

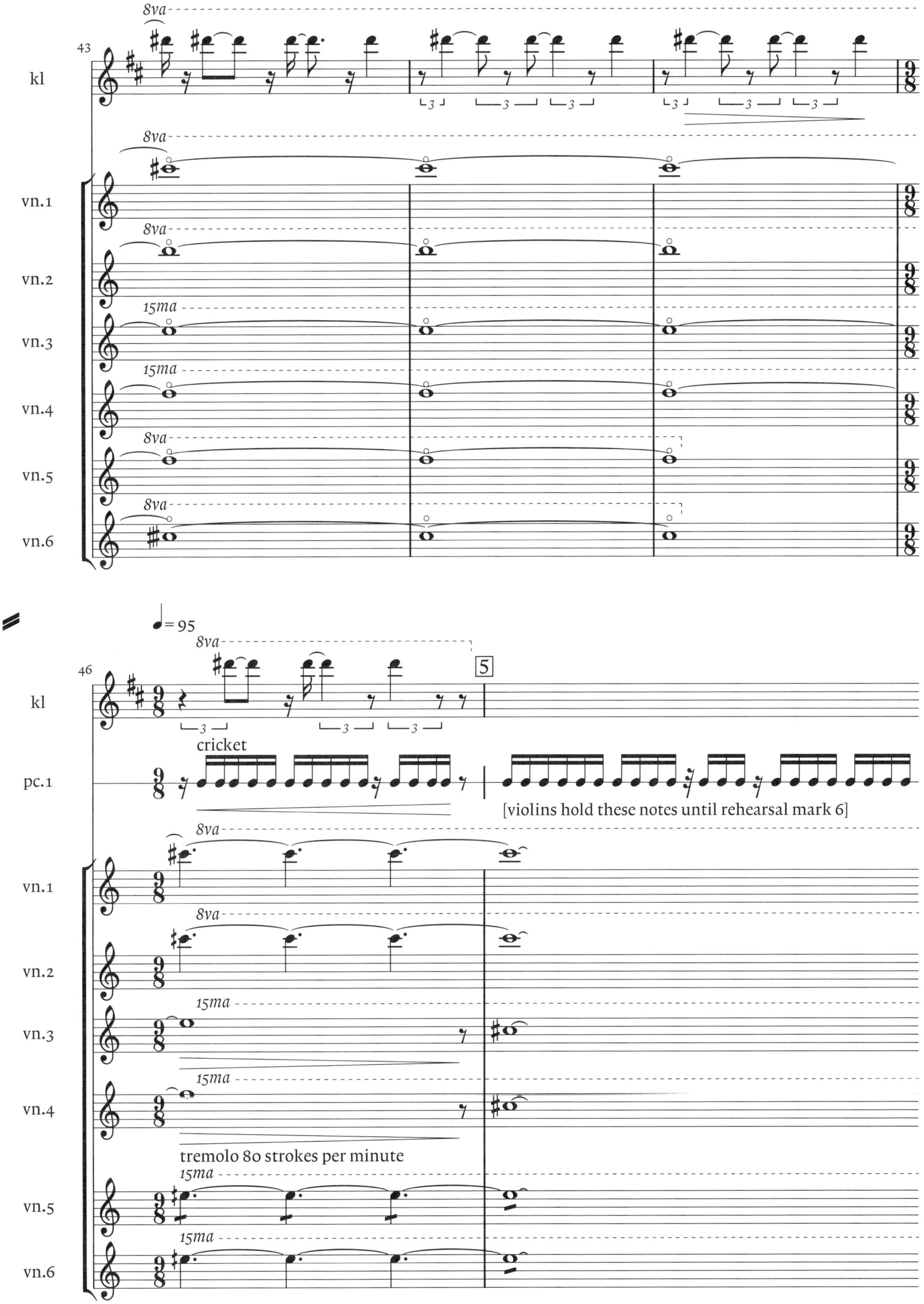

43

kl

8va

vn.1

vn.2

vn.3

vn.4

vn.5

vn.6

15ma

46

♩= 95

5

cricket

pc.1

[violins hold these notes until rehearsal mark 6]

tremolo 80 strokes per minute

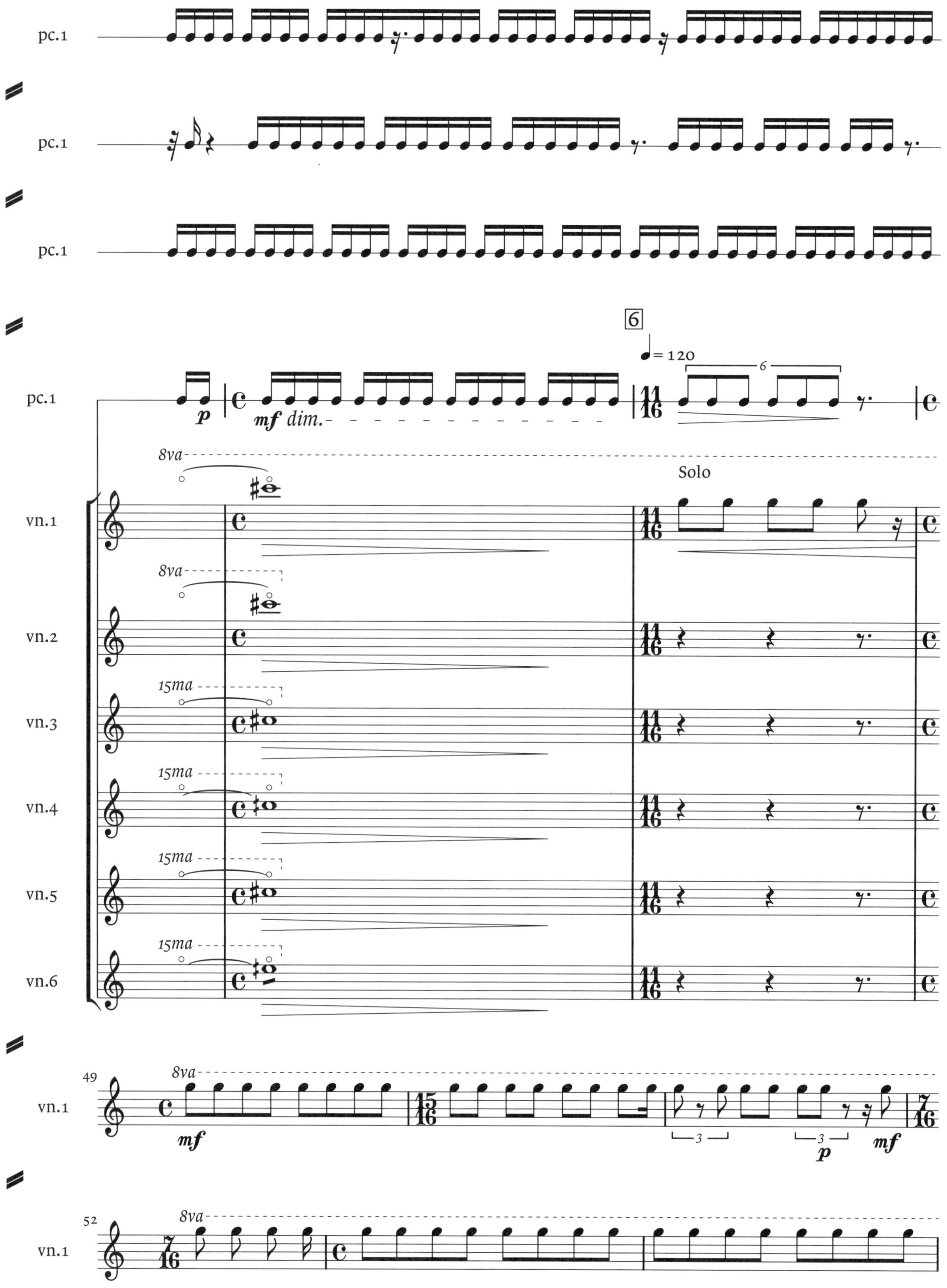
pc.1
pc.1
pc.1
6
= 120
pc.1
p
mf dim.
8va
Solo
vn.1
8va
vn.2
15ma
vn.3
15ma
vn.4
15ma
vn.5
15ma
vn.6
49
vn.1
8va
mf
p
mf
52
vn.1
8va

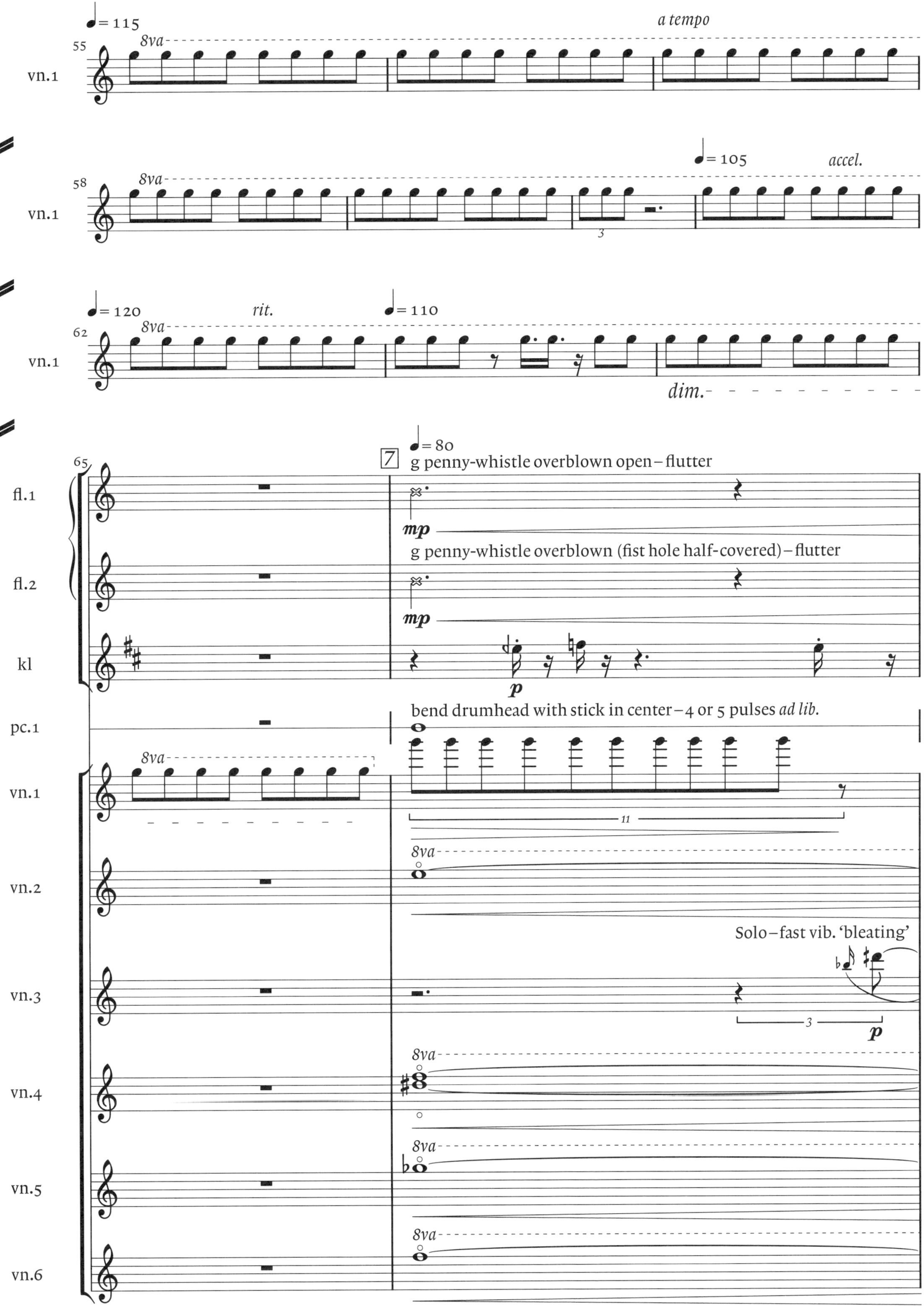

= 115
a tempo
8va
55
vn.1
58
= 105
accel.
3
= 120
rit.
= 110
62
dim.
65
7
= 80
fl.1
g penny-whistle overblown open – flutter
mp
fl.2
g penny-whistle overblown (fist hole half-covered) – flutter
mp
kl
p
pc.1
bend drumhead with stick in center – 4 or 5 pulses ad lib.
11
vn.2
vn.3
Solo – fast vib. 'bleating'
p
vn.4
vn.5
vn.6

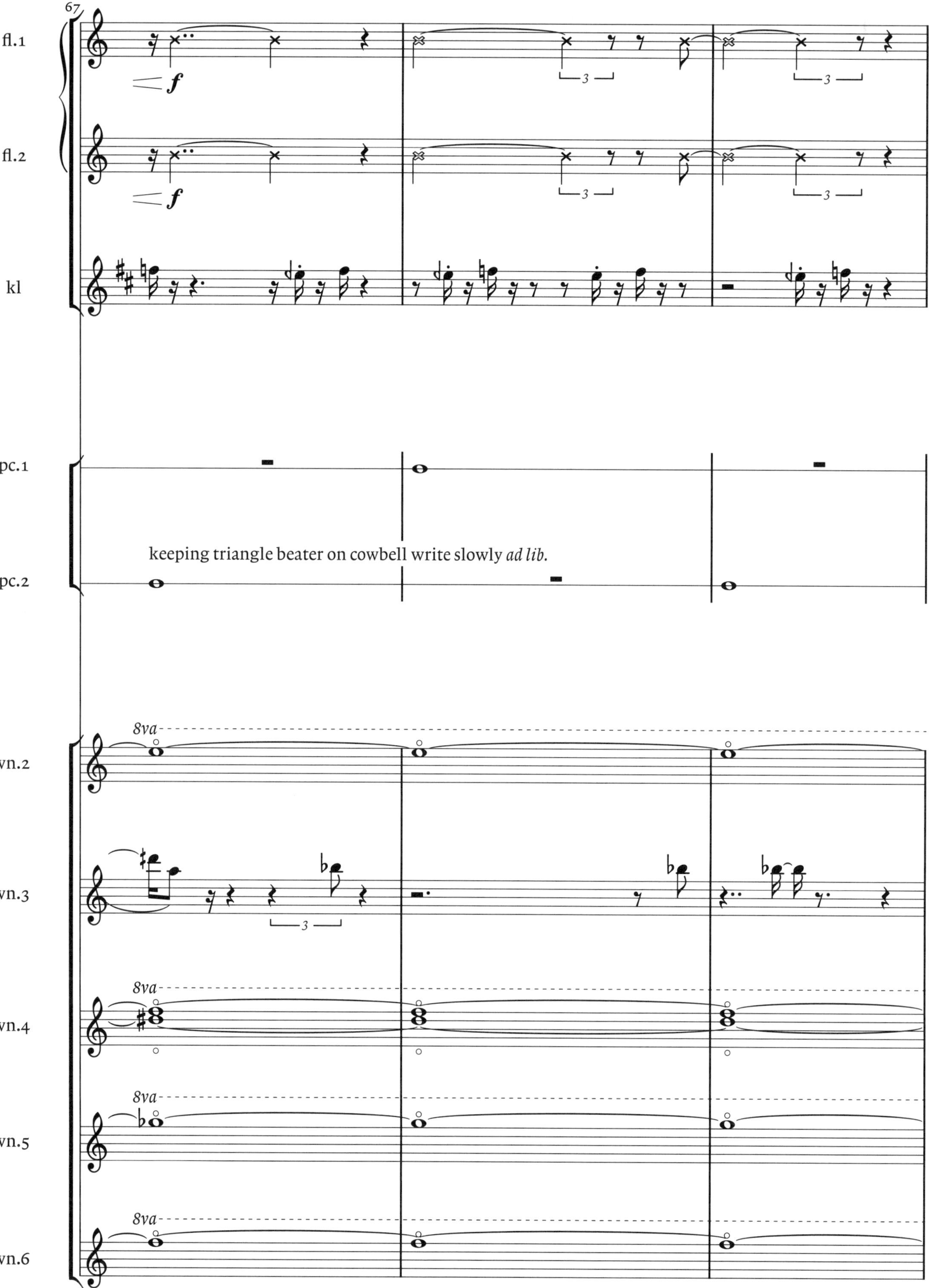
67
fl.1
fl.2
kl
pc.1
pc.2
keeping triangle beater on cowbell write slowly *ad lib.*
vn.2
vn.3
vn.4
vn.5
vn.6
8va

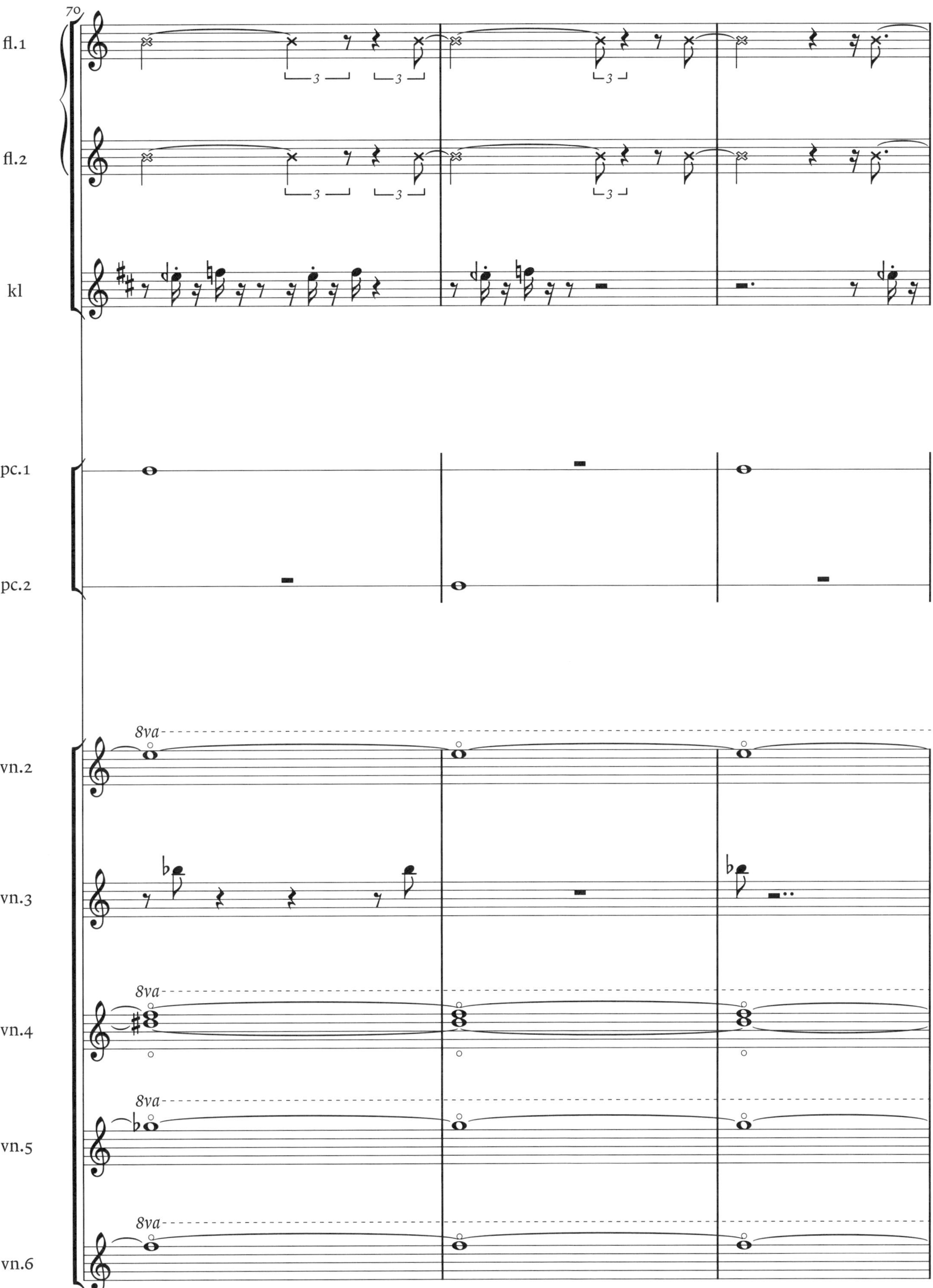
70
fl.1
fl.2
kl
pc.1
pc.2
vn.2
vn.3
vn.4
vn.5
vn.6
8va
8va
8va
8va
3
3
3
3
3
3

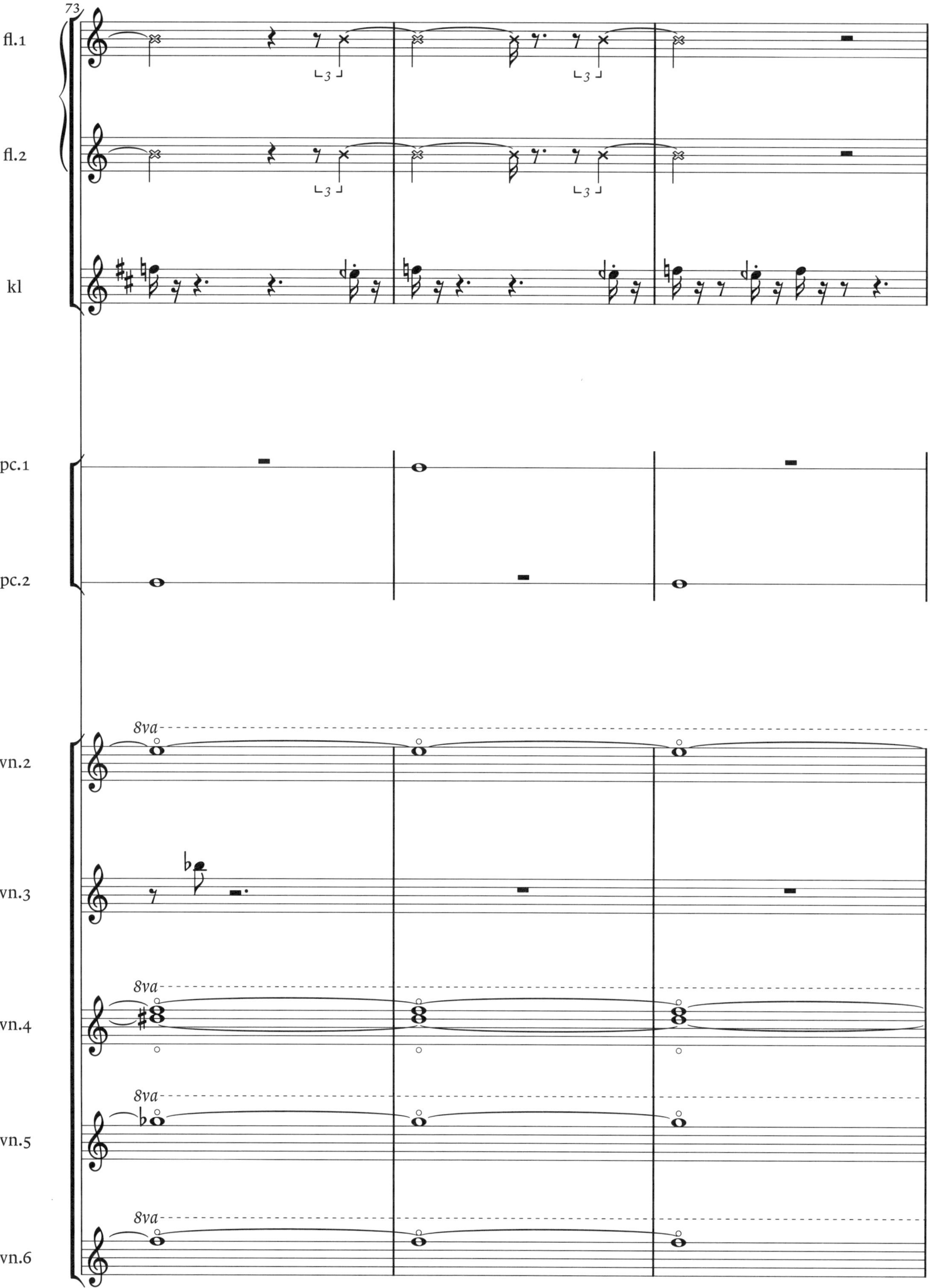
73
fl.1
fl.2
kl
pc.1
pc.2
vn.2
vn.3
vn.4
vn.5
vn.6
8va
8va
8va
8va

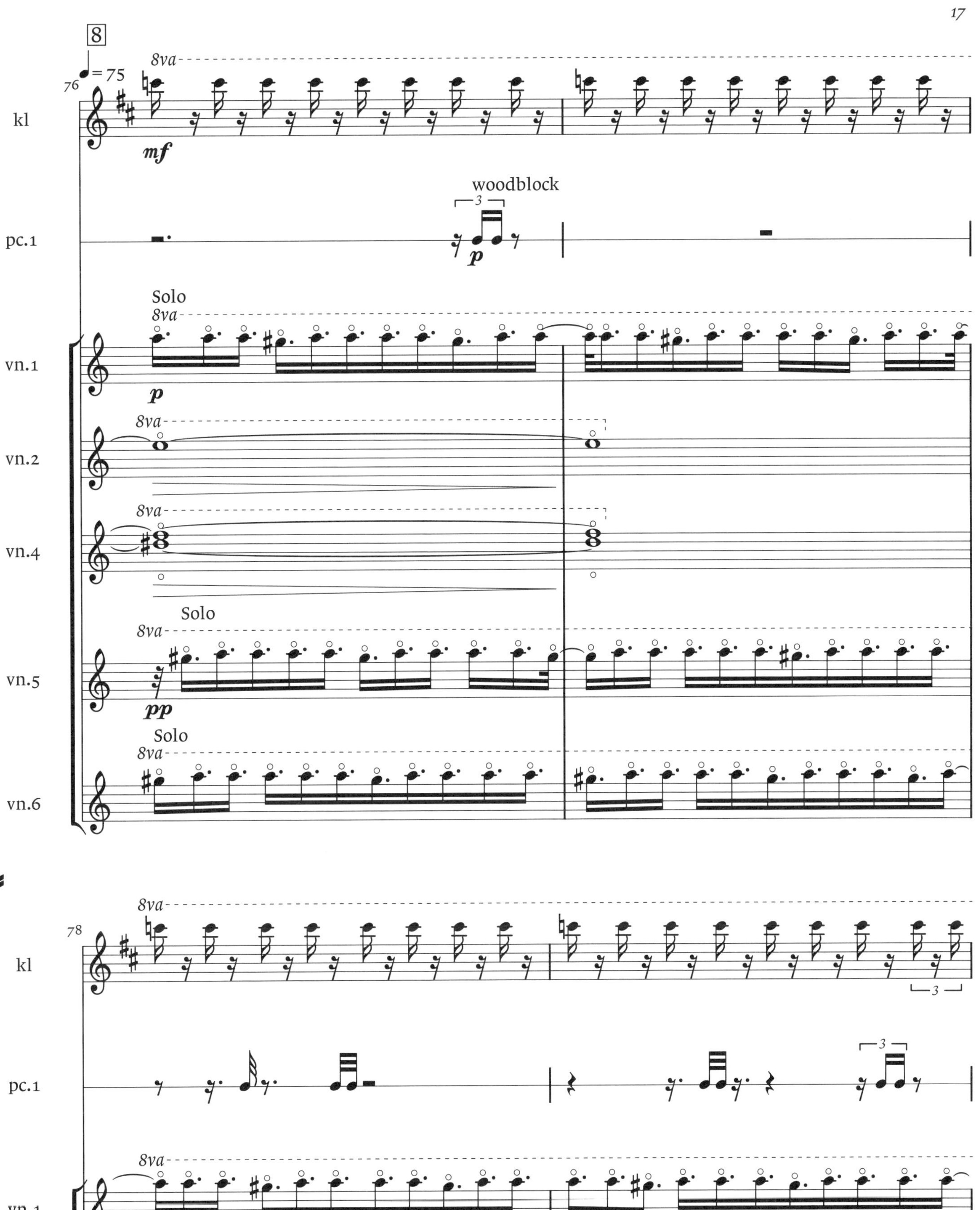
8
♩=75
76
kl
8va
mf
pc.1
woodblock
3
p
Solo
vn.1
p
vn.2
vn.4
Solo
vn.5
pp
Solo
vn.6
78
kl
pc.1
vn.1
vn.5
vn.6

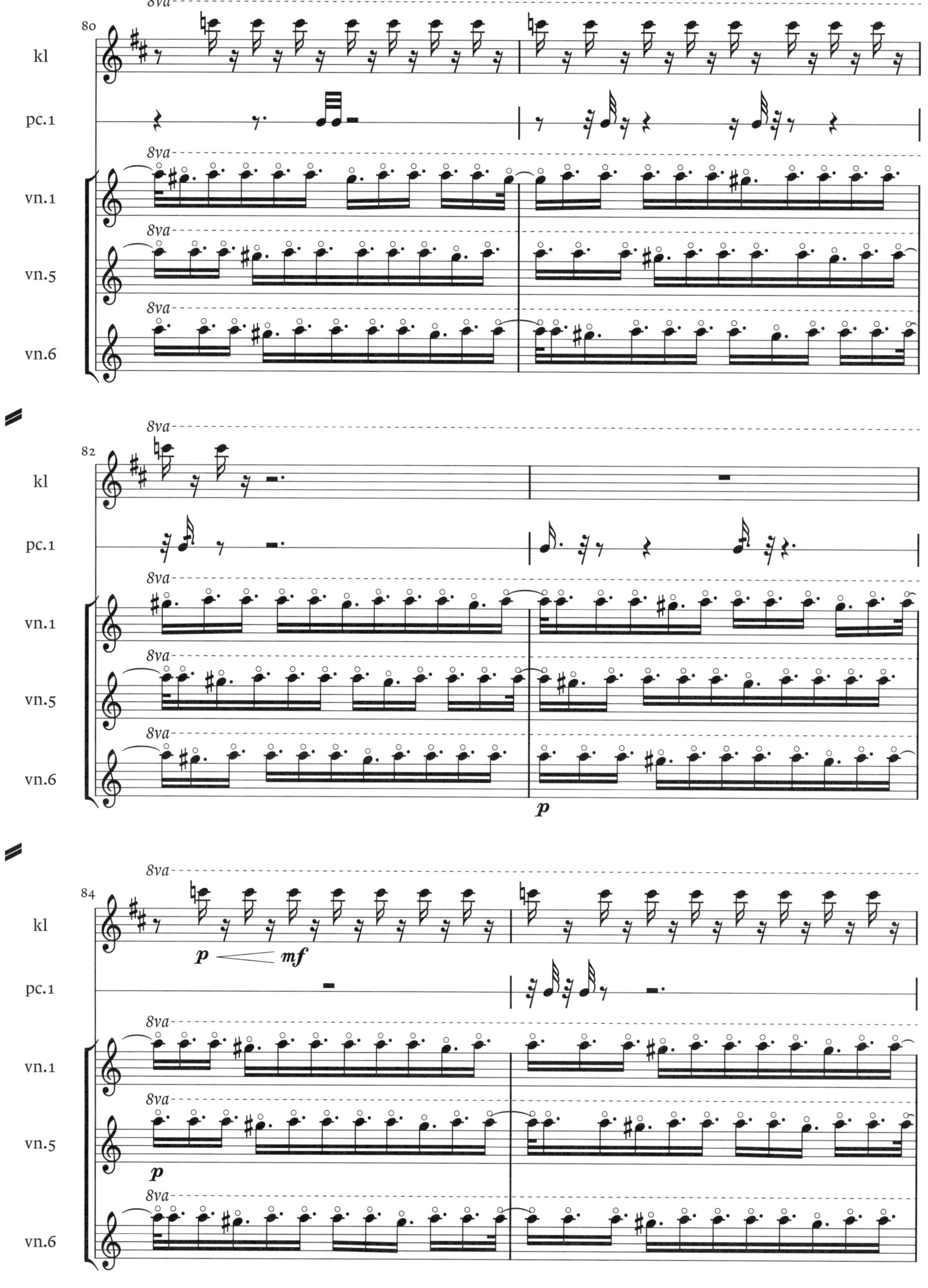
8va
80
kl
pc.1
vn.1
vn.5
vn.6
82
p
84
p
mf

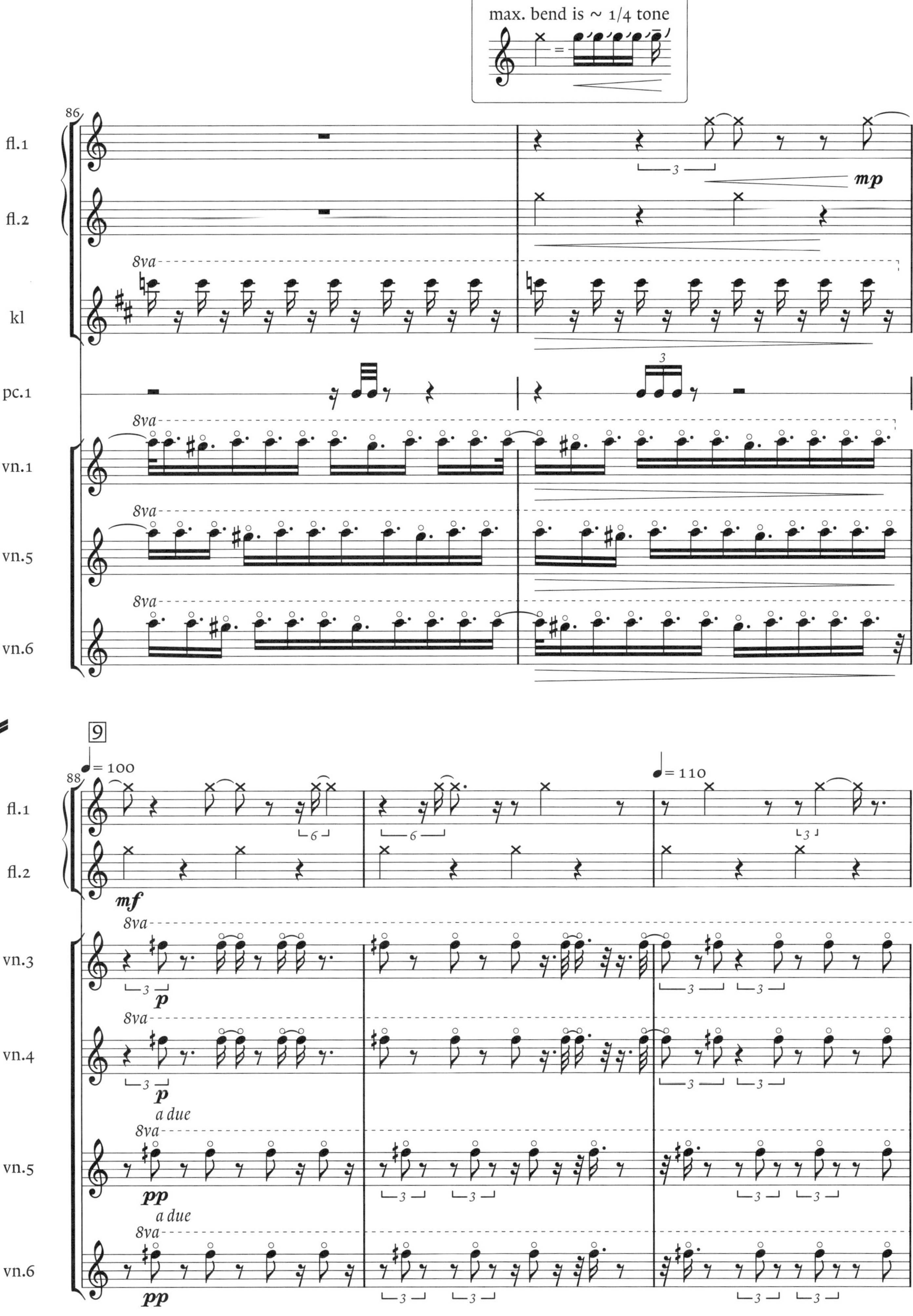
max. bend is ~ 1/4 tone
fl.1
fl.2
kl
pc.1
vn.1
vn.5
vn.6
8va
mp
9
♩= 100
♩= 110
vn.3
vn.4
mf
p
pp
a due

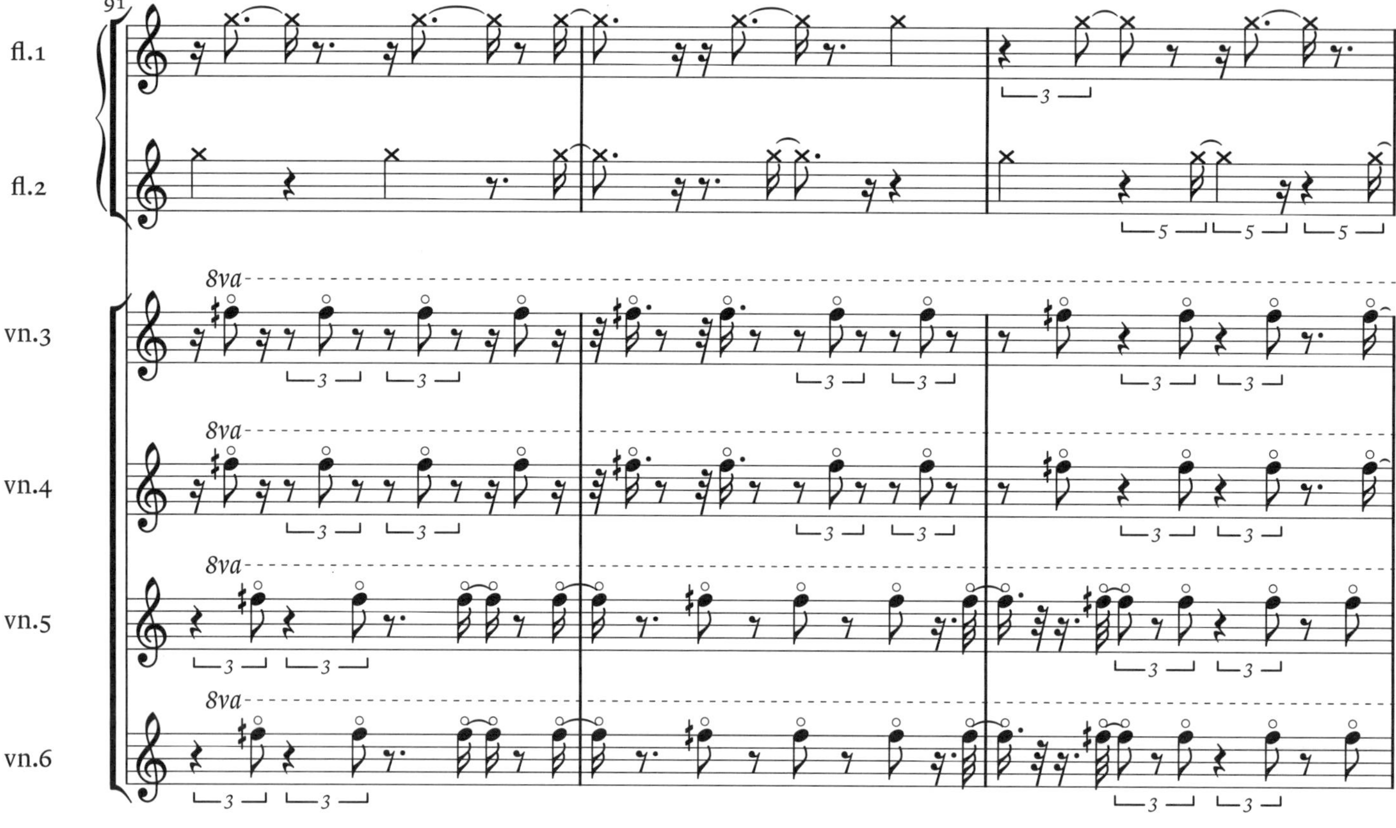
91
fl.1
fl.2
vn.3
vn.4
vn.5
vn.6
8va

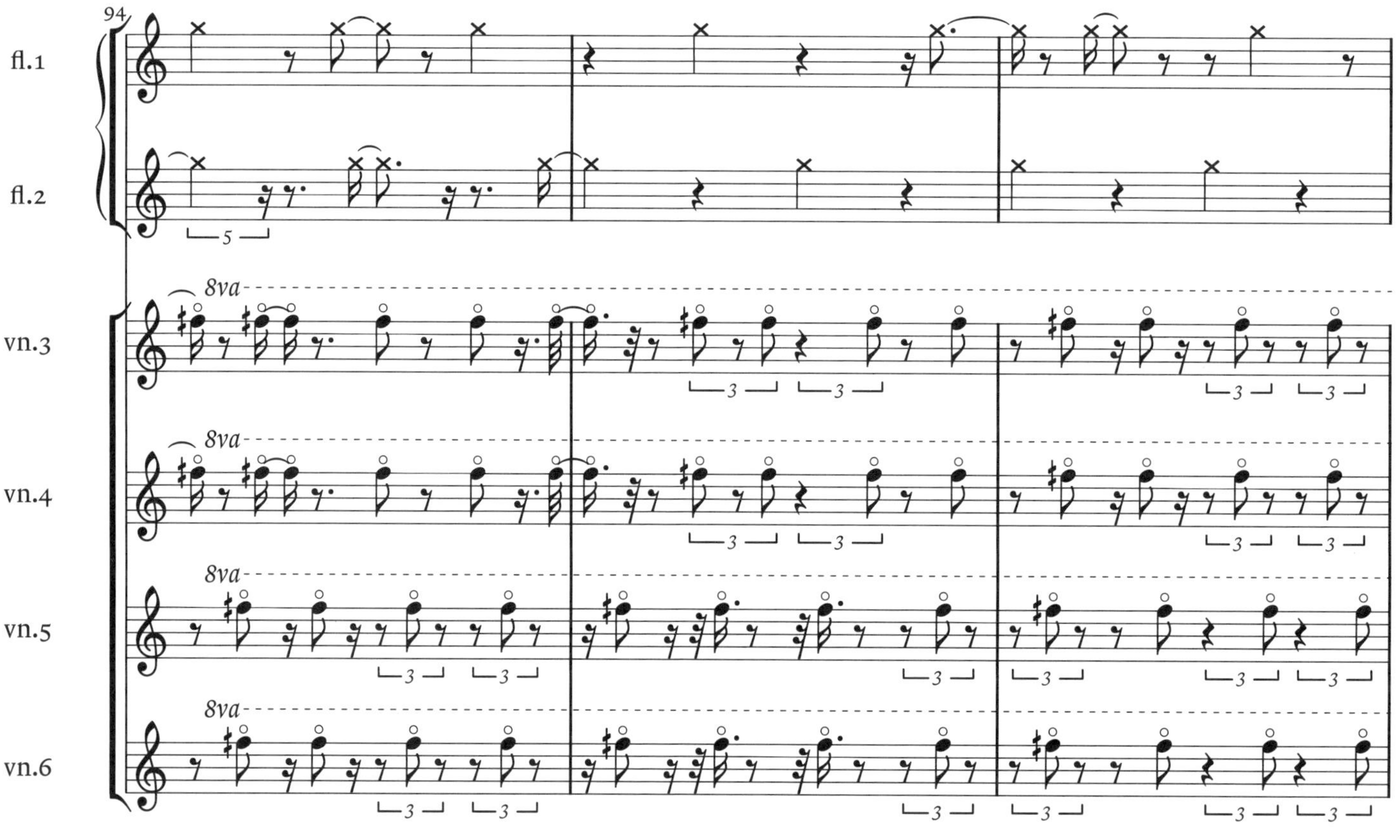
94
fl.1
fl.2
vn.3
vn.4
vn.5
vn.6
8va

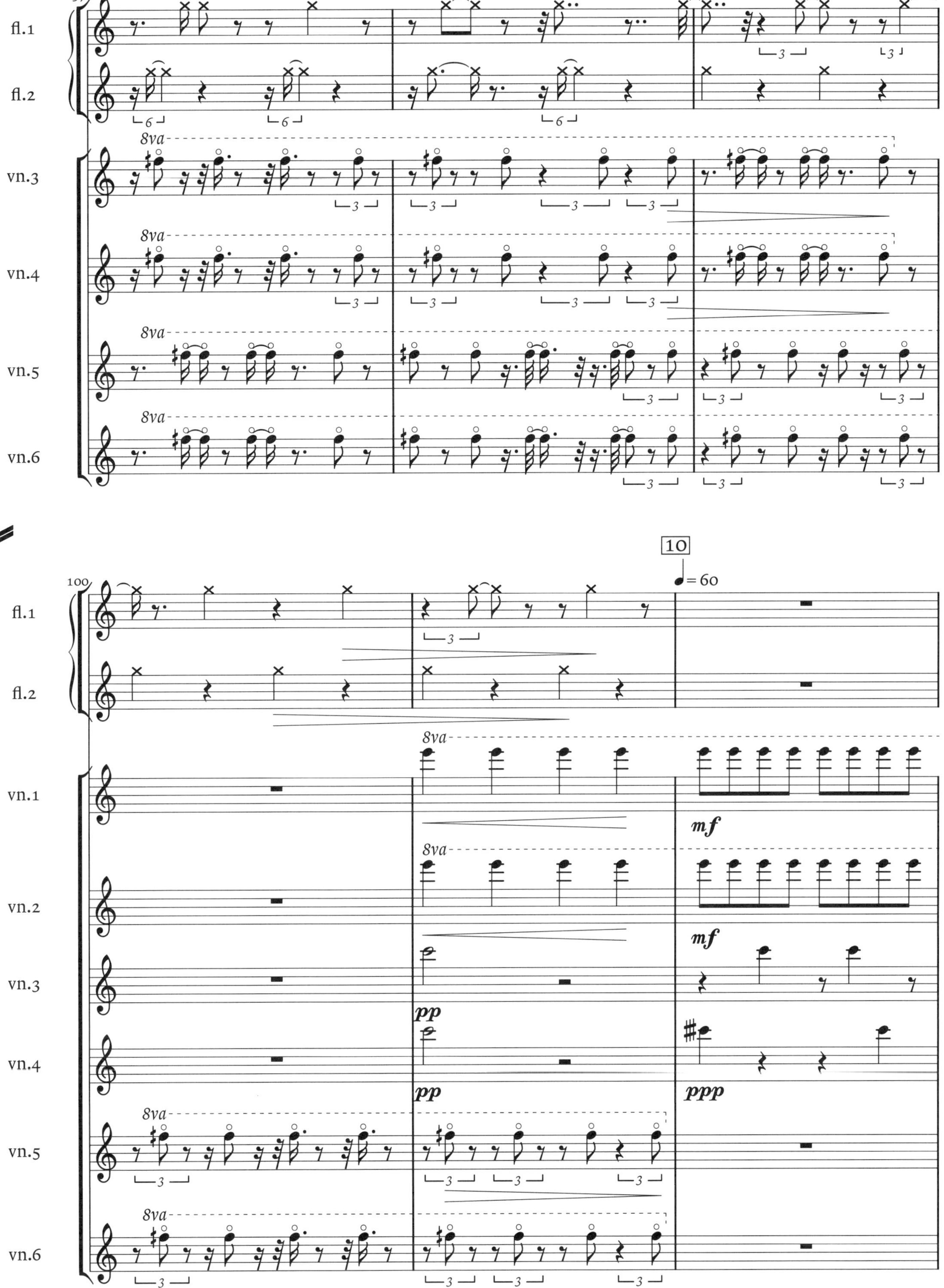
97
fl.1
fl.2
vn.3
vn.4
vn.5
vn.6
8va
100
10
♩= 60
vn.1
vn.2
mf
pp
ppp

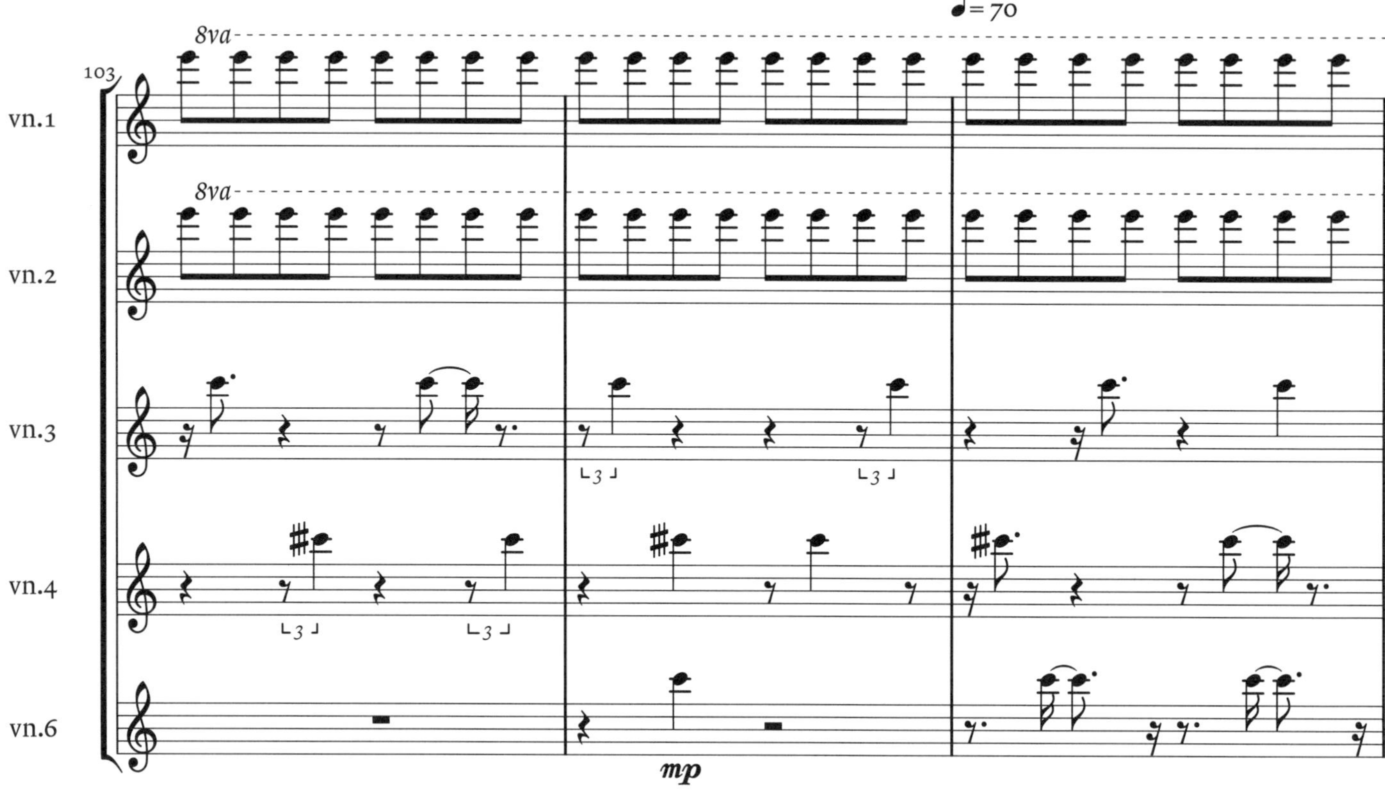
♩= 70
8va
103
vn.1
vn.2
vn.3
vn.4
vn.6
mp

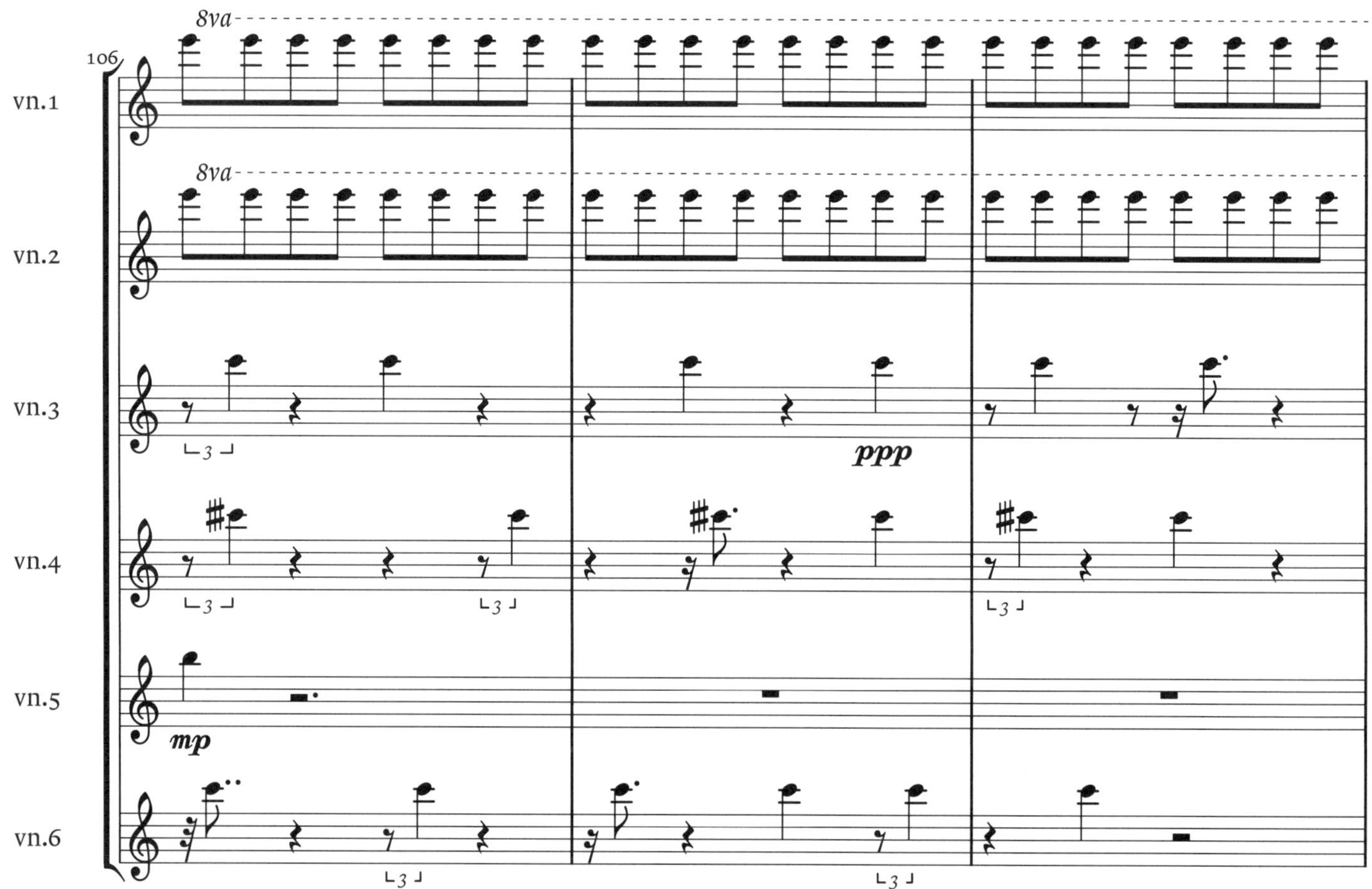
8va
106
vn.1
vn.2
vn.3
vn.4
vn.5
vn.6
ppp
mp

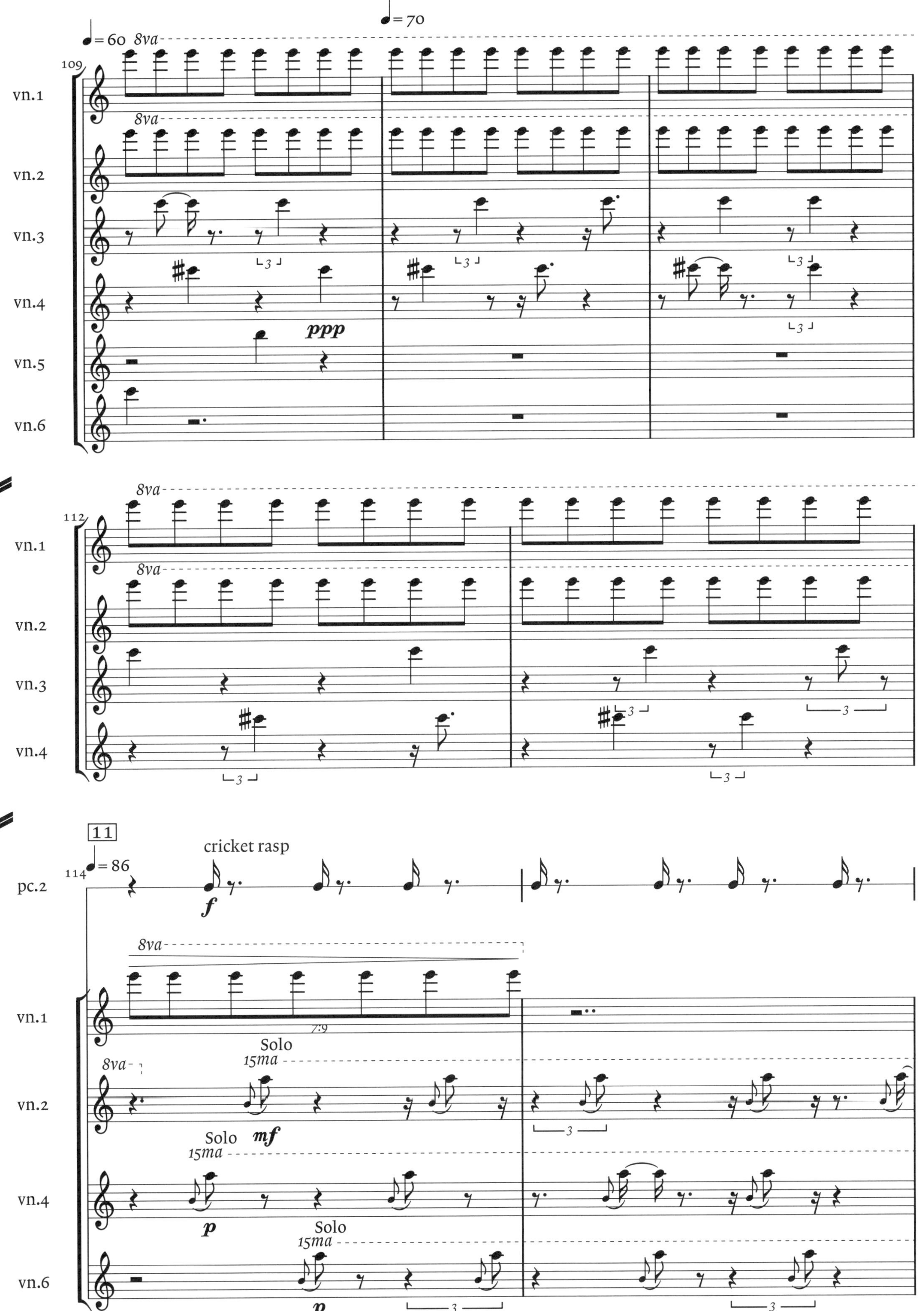

♩= 60
♩= 70
8va
109
vn.1
vn.2
vn.3
vn.4
vn.5
vn.6
ppp
112
11
cricket rasp
♩= 86
114
pc.2
f
7:9
Solo
15ma
mf
p

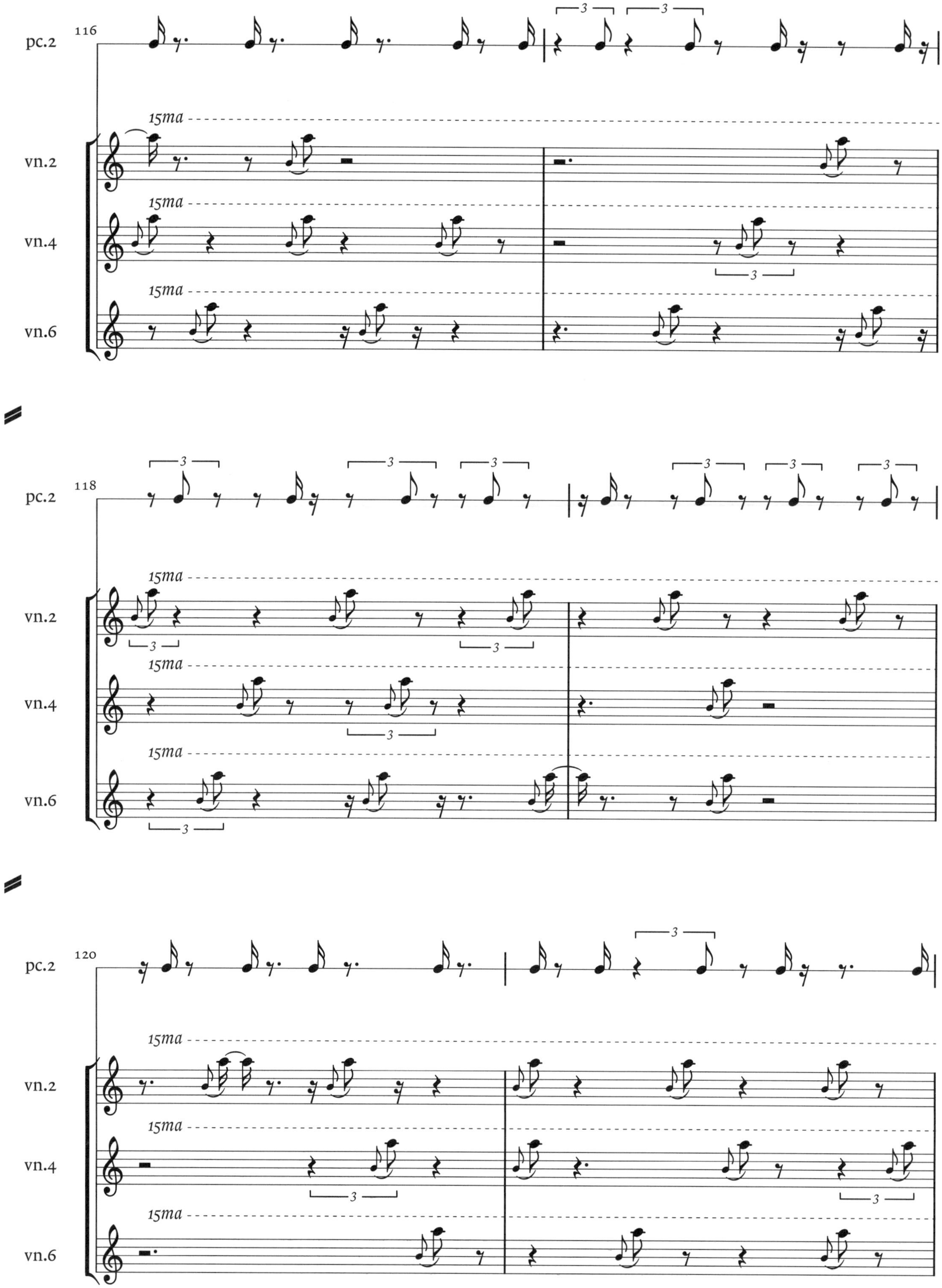

116
pc.2
15ma
vn.2
15ma
vn.4
15ma
vn.6

118
pc.2
15ma
vn.2
15ma
vn.4
15ma
vn.6

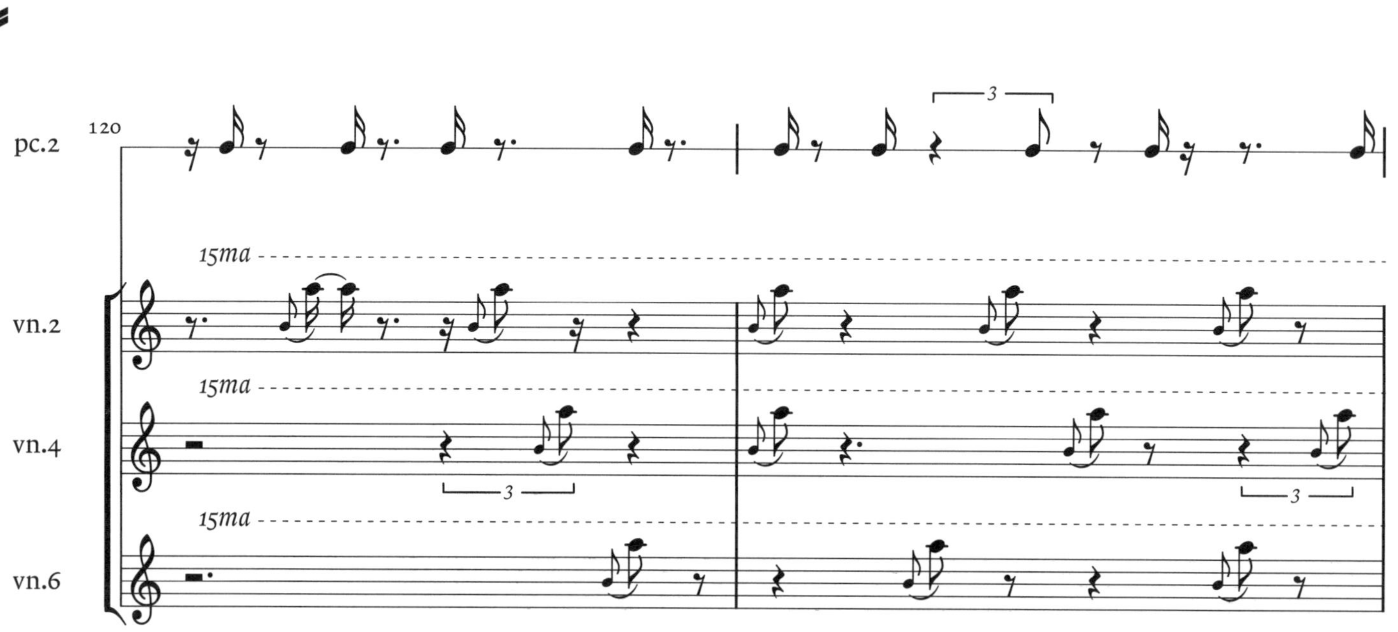

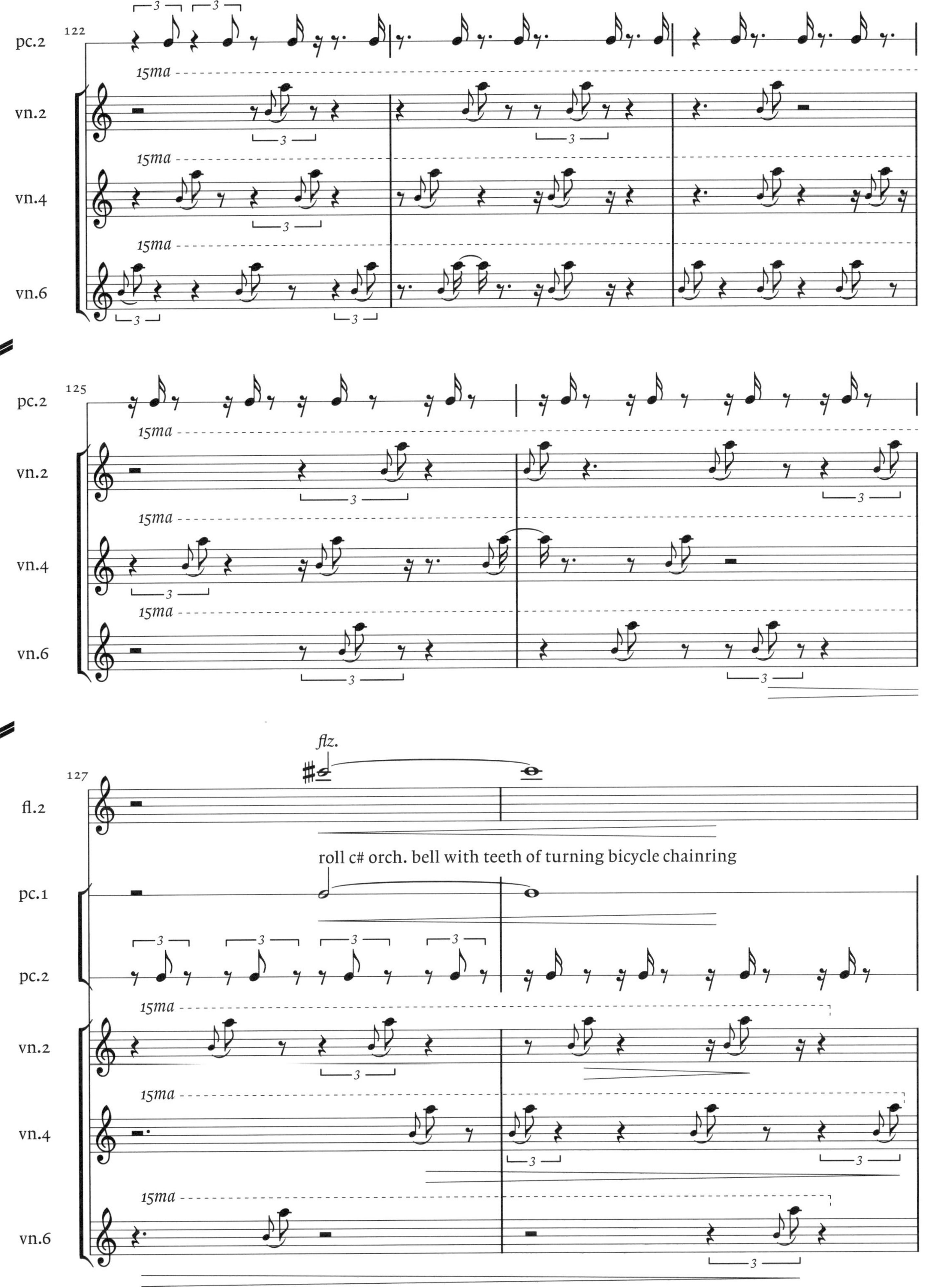
122
pc.2
vn.2
vn.4
vn.6
15ma
125
127
fl.2
flz.
roll c# orch. bell with teeth of turning bicycle chainring
pc.1

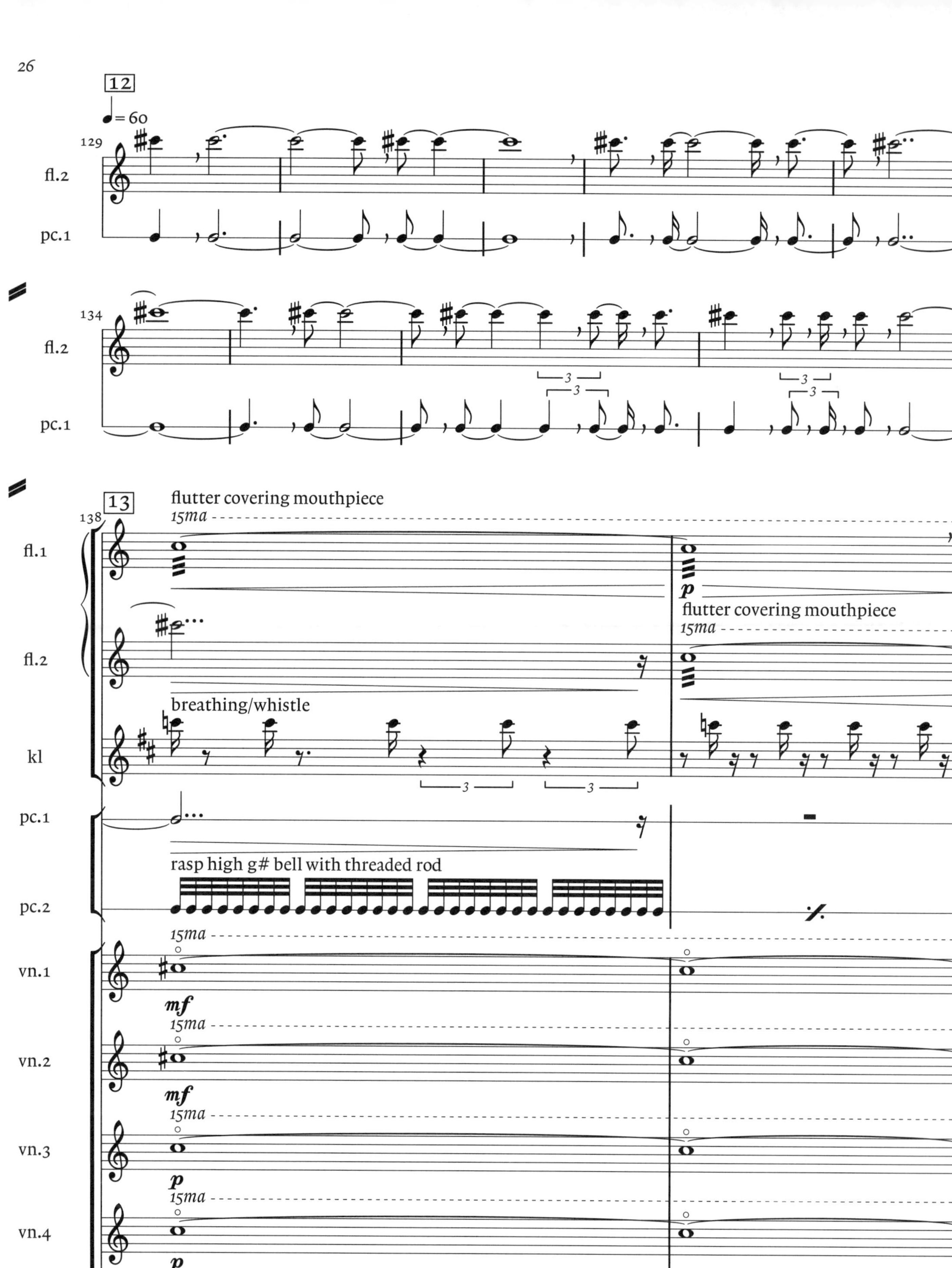
12
♩= 60
129
fl.2
pc.1
134
fl.2
pc.1
13
138
flutter covering mouthpiece
15ma
fl.1
p
flutter covering mouthpiece
15ma
fl.2
breathing/whistle
kl
pc.1
rasp high g# bell with threaded rod
pc.2
15ma
vn.1
mf
15ma
vn.2
mf
15ma
vn.3
p
15ma
vn.4
p
15ma
vn.5
mp
15ma
vn.6
pp

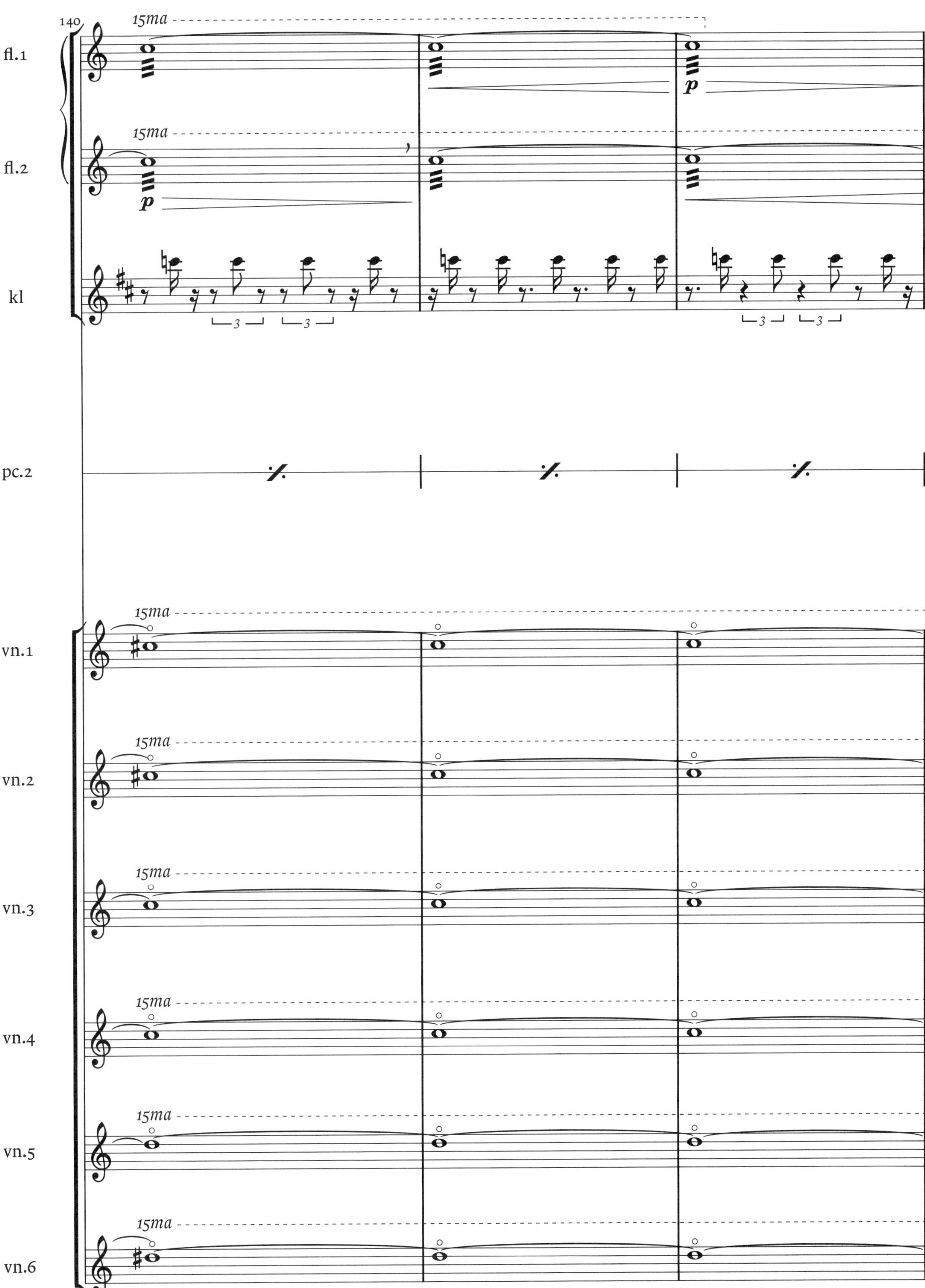
140
fl.1
fl.2
kl
pc.2
vn.1
vn.2
vn.3
vn.4
vn.5
vn.6
15ma
p
3

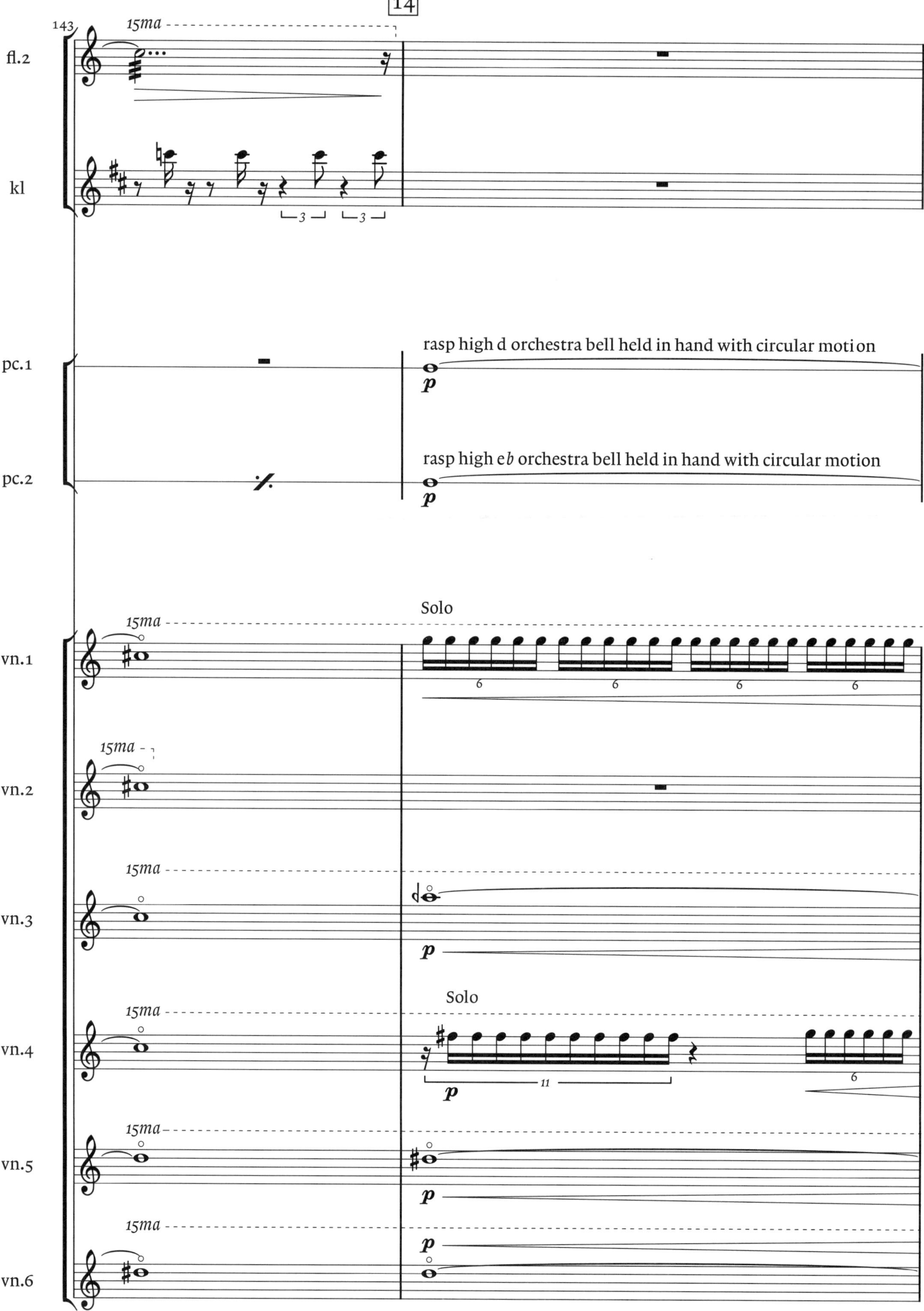
14
143
15ma
fl.2
kl
pc.1
rasp high d orchestra bell held in hand with circular motion
pc.2
rasp high e♭ orchestra bell held in hand with circular motion
Solo
vn.1
vn.2
vn.3
vn.4
vn.5
vn.6

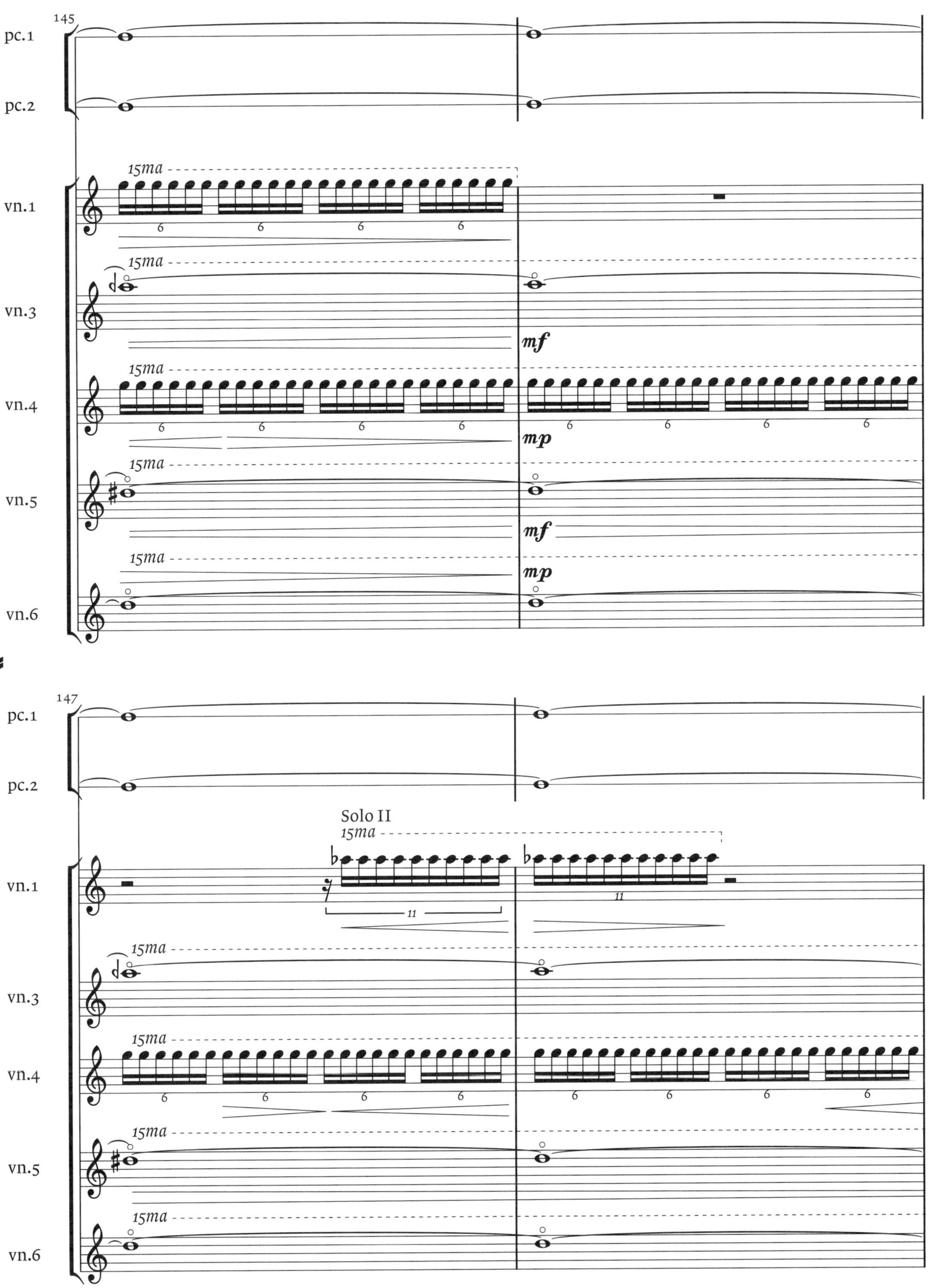
145
pc.1
pc.2
vn.1
vn.3
vn.4
vn.5
vn.6
15ma
mf
mp
147
Solo II
11

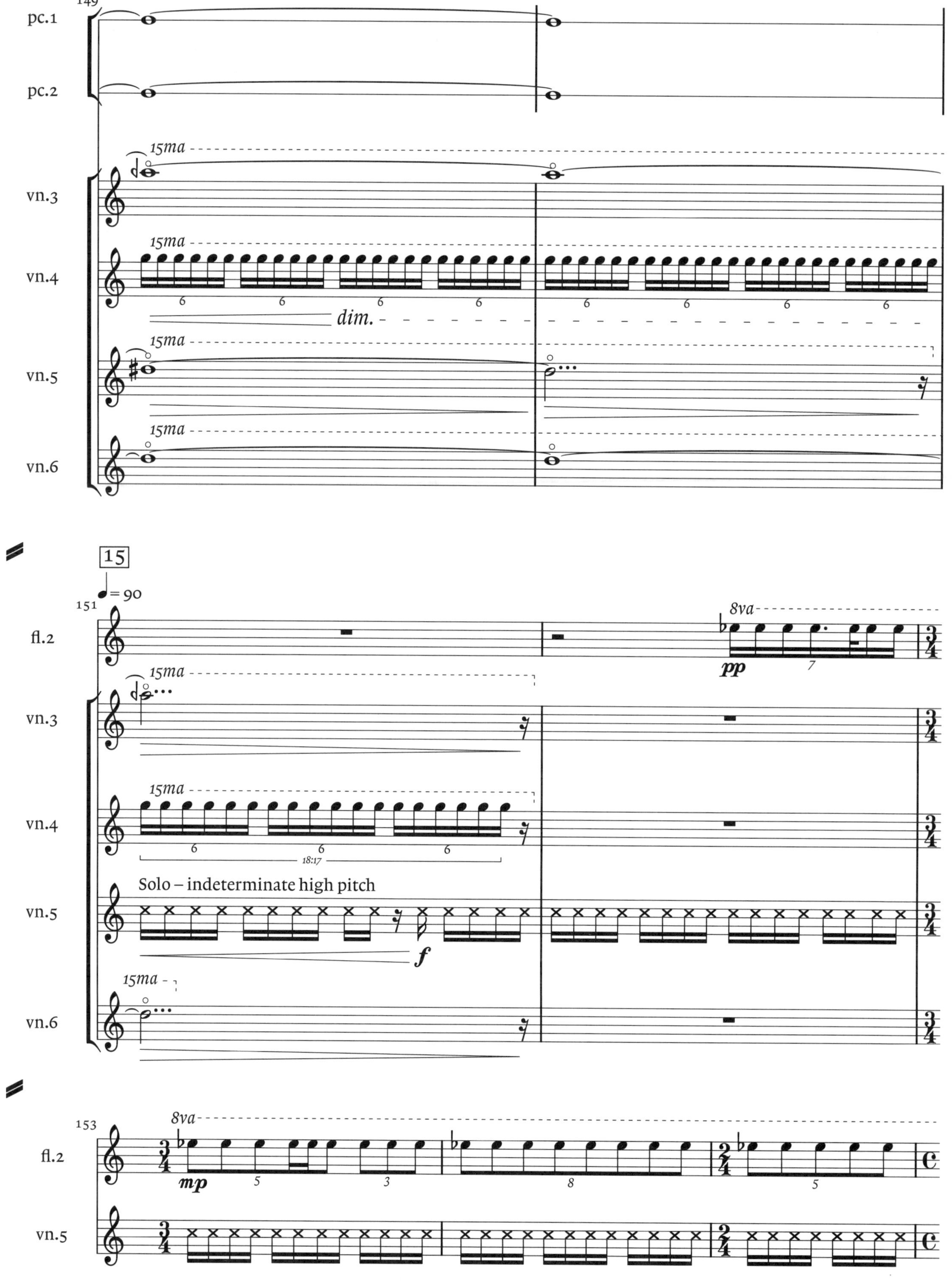
149
pc.1
pc.2
15ma
vn.3
vn.4
6
dim.
vn.5
vn.6
15
♩= 90
151
fl.2
8va
pp
7
Solo – indeterminate high pitch
18:17
f
153
mp
5
3
8
vn.5

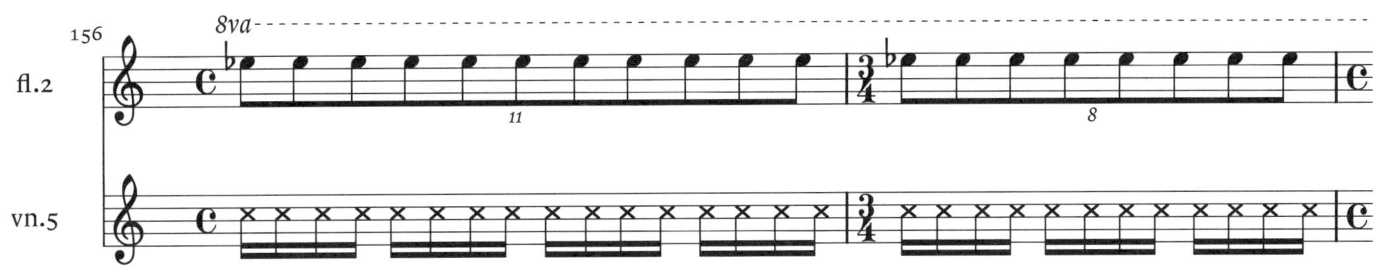
156
fl.2
8va
11
8
vn.5

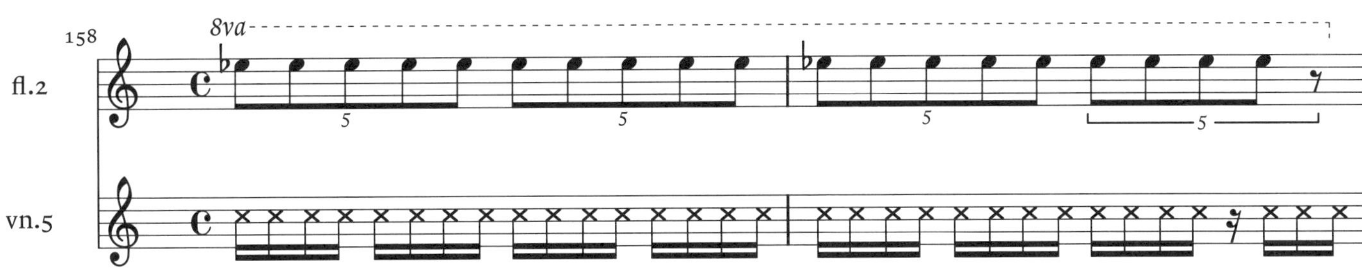
158
fl.2
8va
5
5
5
5
vn.5

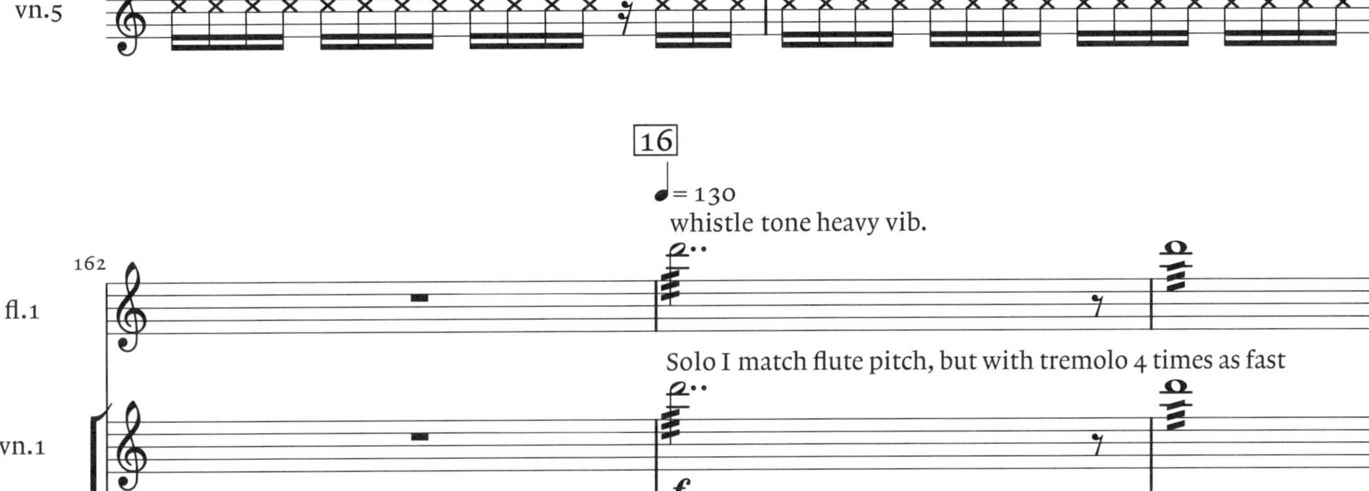
160
vn.5
16
♩= 130
whistle tone heavy vib.
162
fl.1
Solo I match flute pitch, but with tremolo 4 times as fast
vn.1
f
vn.5

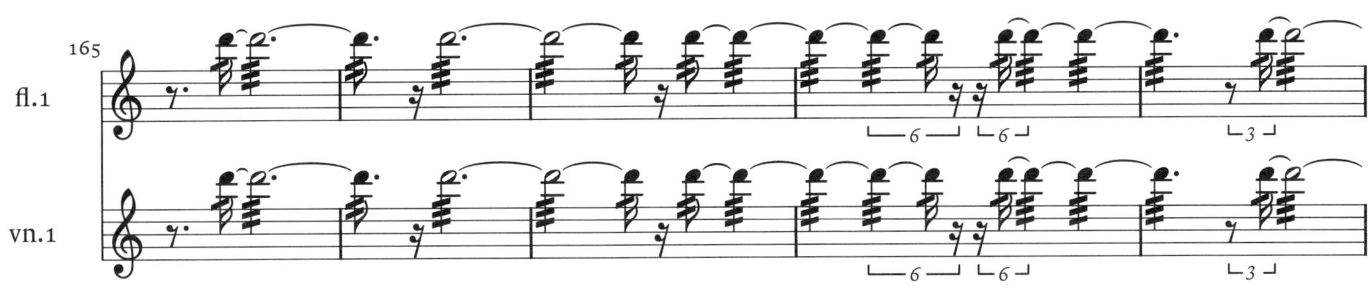
165
fl.1
6
6
3
vn.1
6
6
3

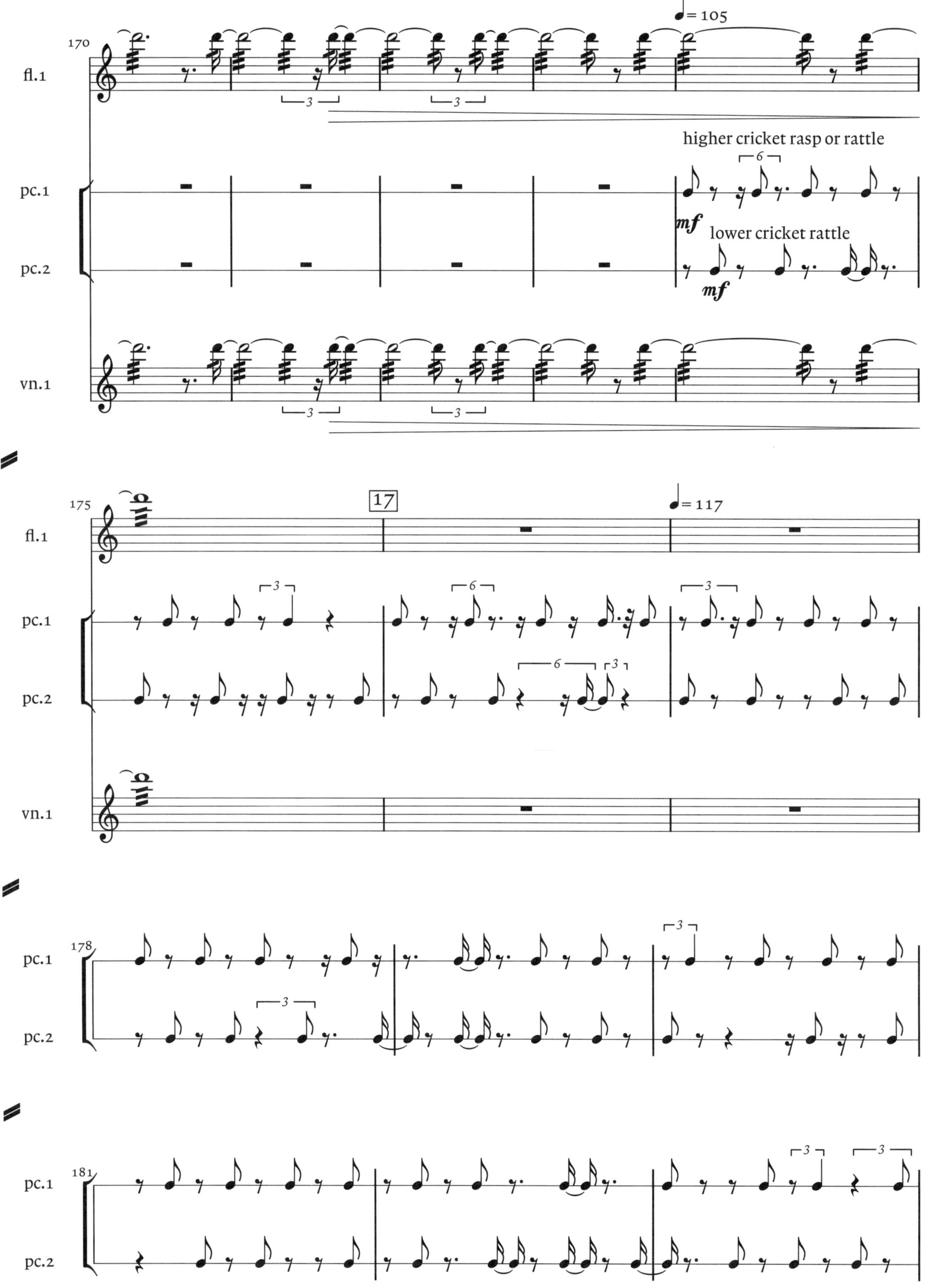

170
fl.1
pc.1
pc.2
vn.1
♩= 105
higher cricket rasp or rattle
mf
lower cricket rattle
mf
175
17
♩= 117
178
181

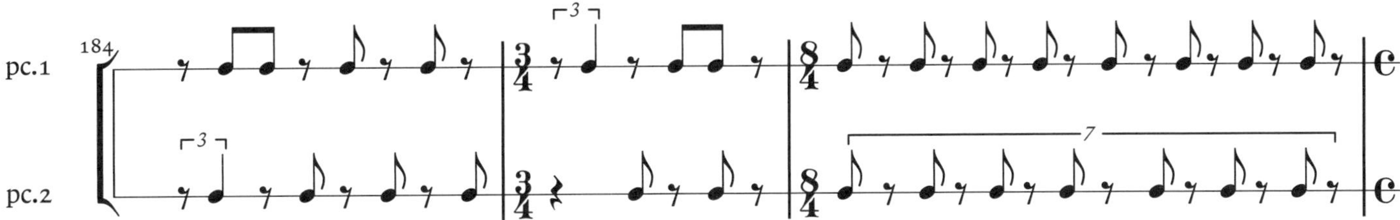
184
pc.1
pc.2
3
3
7

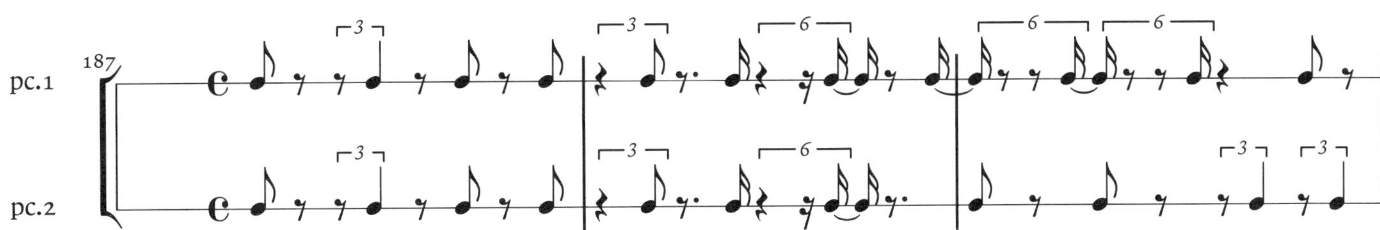
187
pc.1
pc.2
3
6
6
6
3
6
3
3

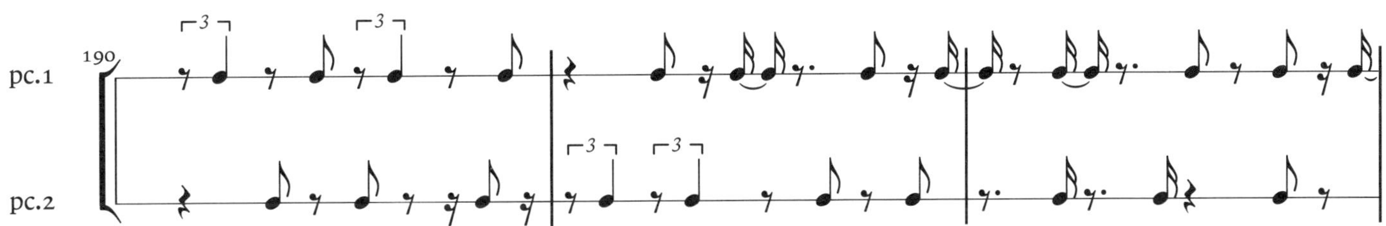
190
pc.1
pc.2
3
3
3
3

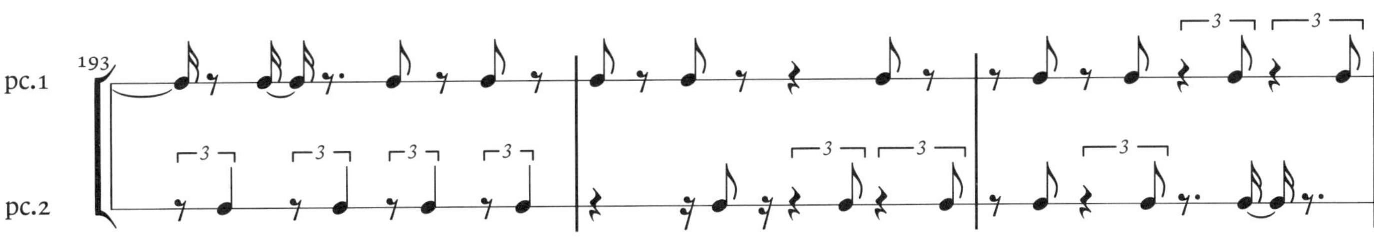
193
pc.1
pc.2
3
3
3
3
3
3
3
3
3

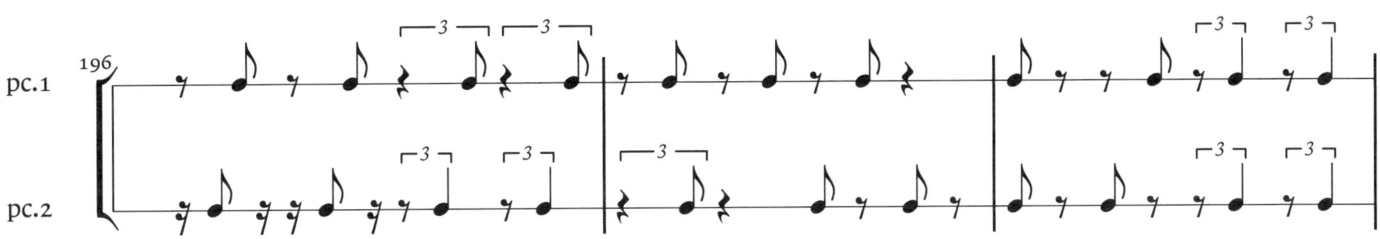
196
pc.1
pc.2
3
3
3
3
3
3
3
3
3

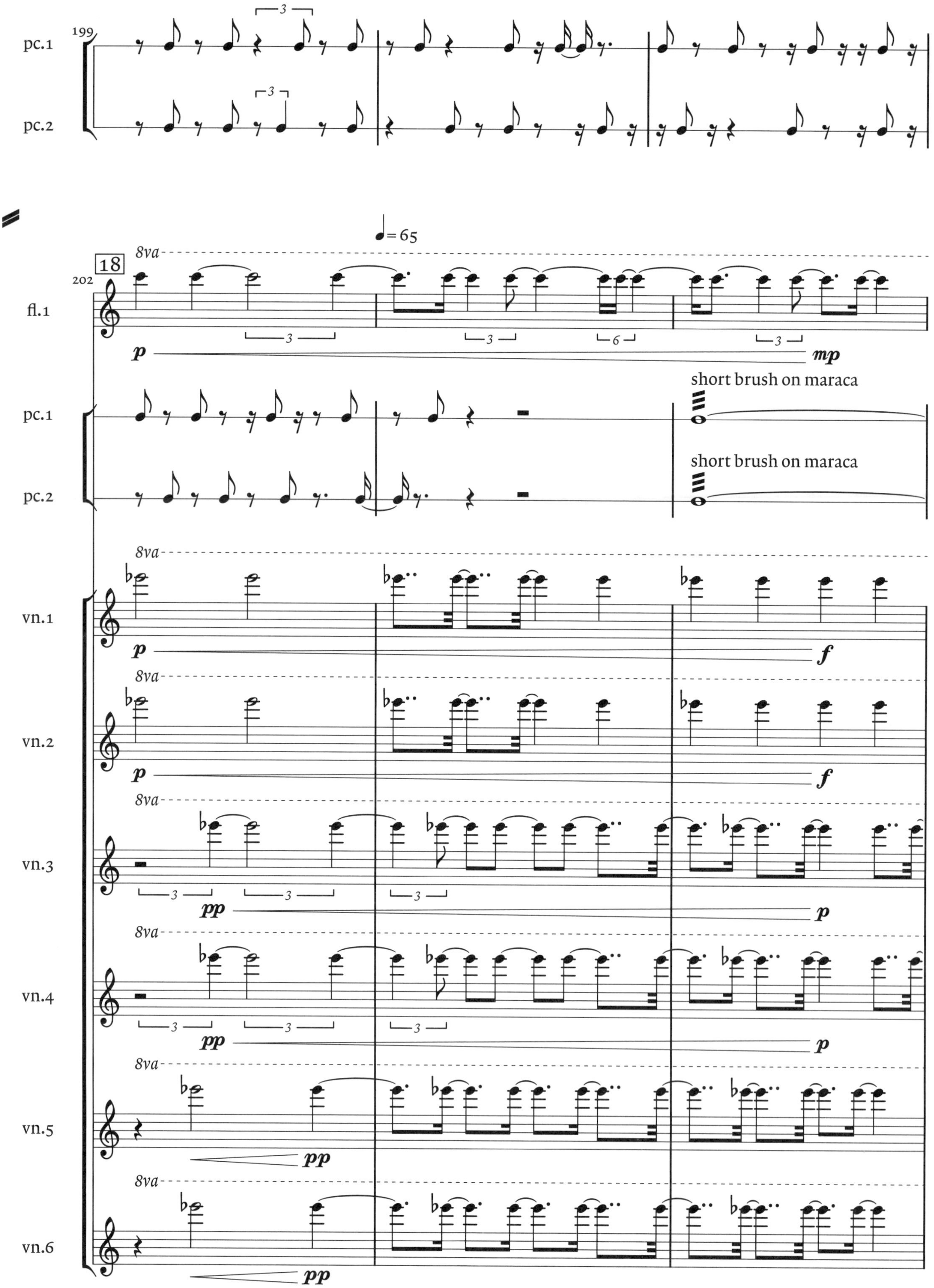

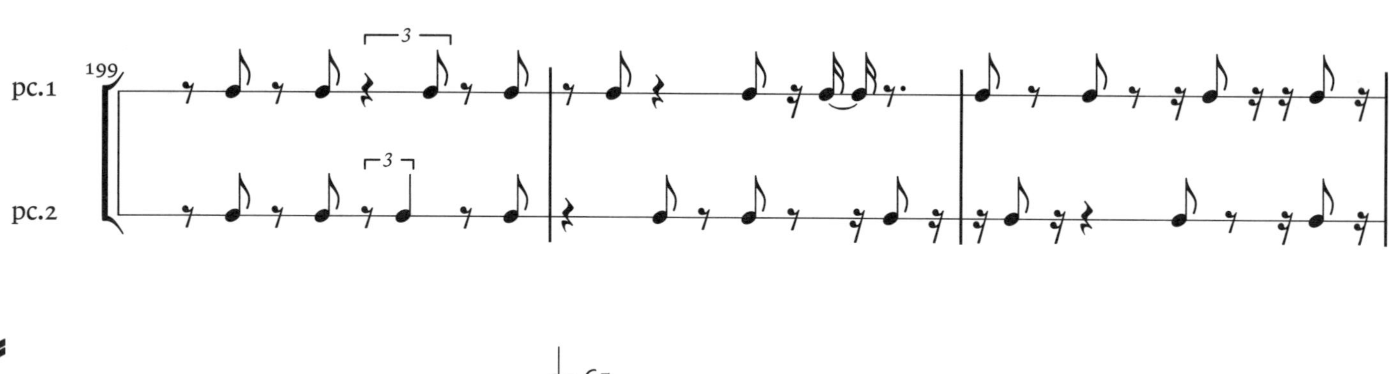

♩= 65

18

202

fl.1 8va
p mp

pc.1 short brush on maraca

pc.2 short brush on maraca

vn.1 8va
p f

vn.2 8va
p f

vn.3 8va
pp p

vn.4 8va
pp p

vn.5 8va
pp

vn.6 8va
pp

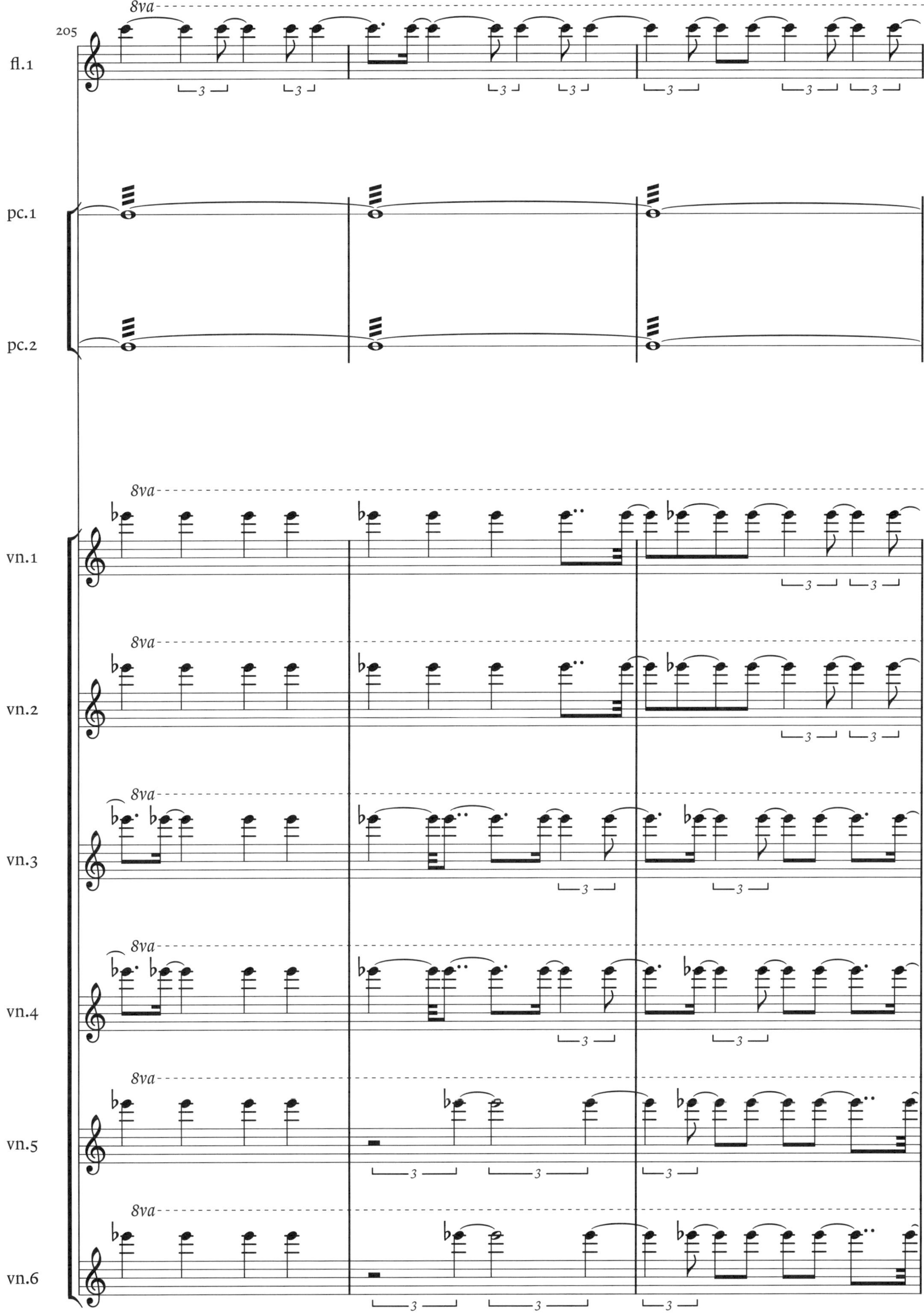
205
fl.1
8va
pc.1
pc.2
vn.1
8va
vn.2
8va
vn.3
8va
vn.4
8va
vn.5
8va
vn.6
8va

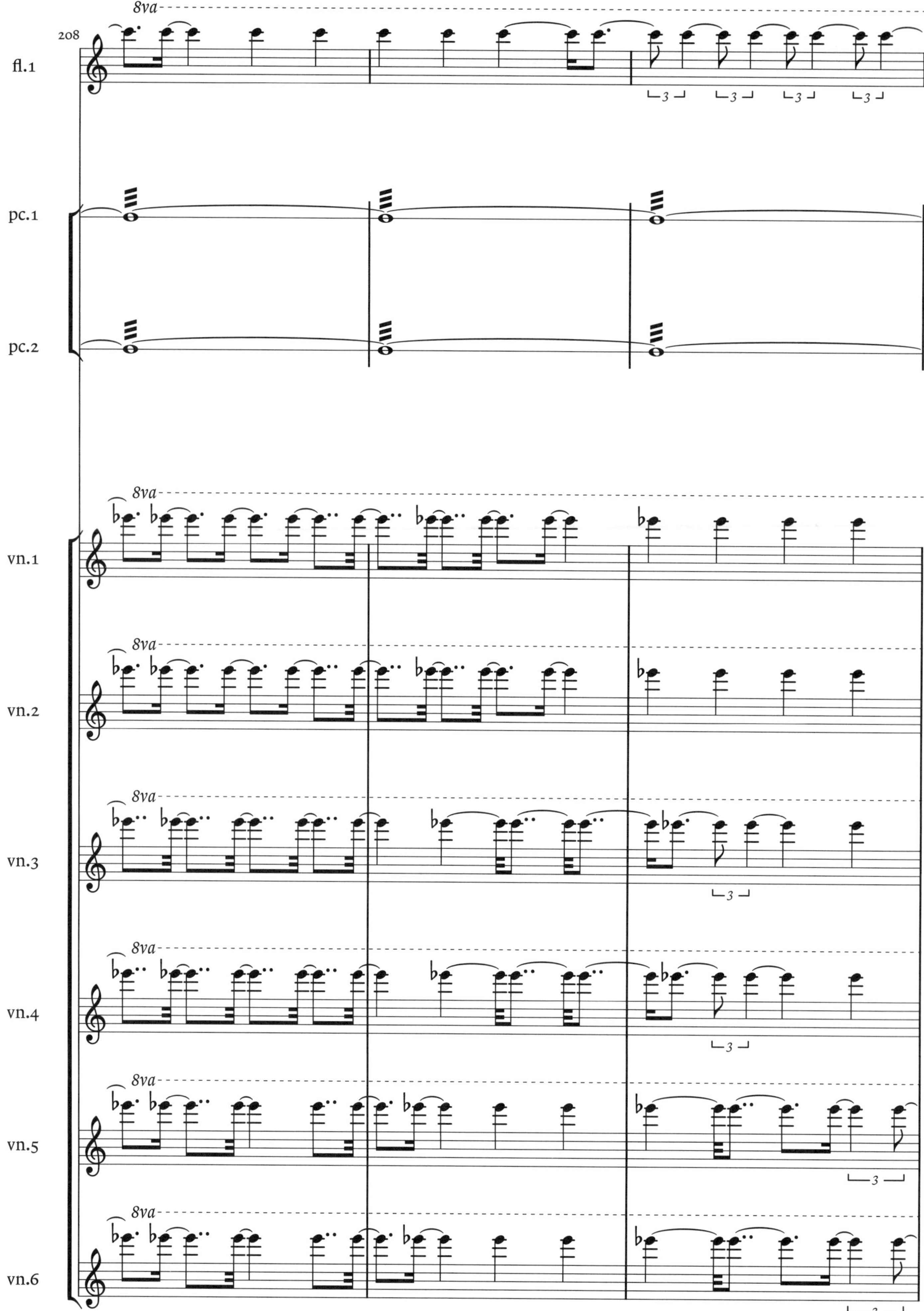
208
8va
fl.1
3
3
3
3
pc.1
pc.2
8va
vn.1
8va
vn.2
8va
vn.3
3
8va
vn.4
3
8va
vn.5
3
8va
vn.6
3

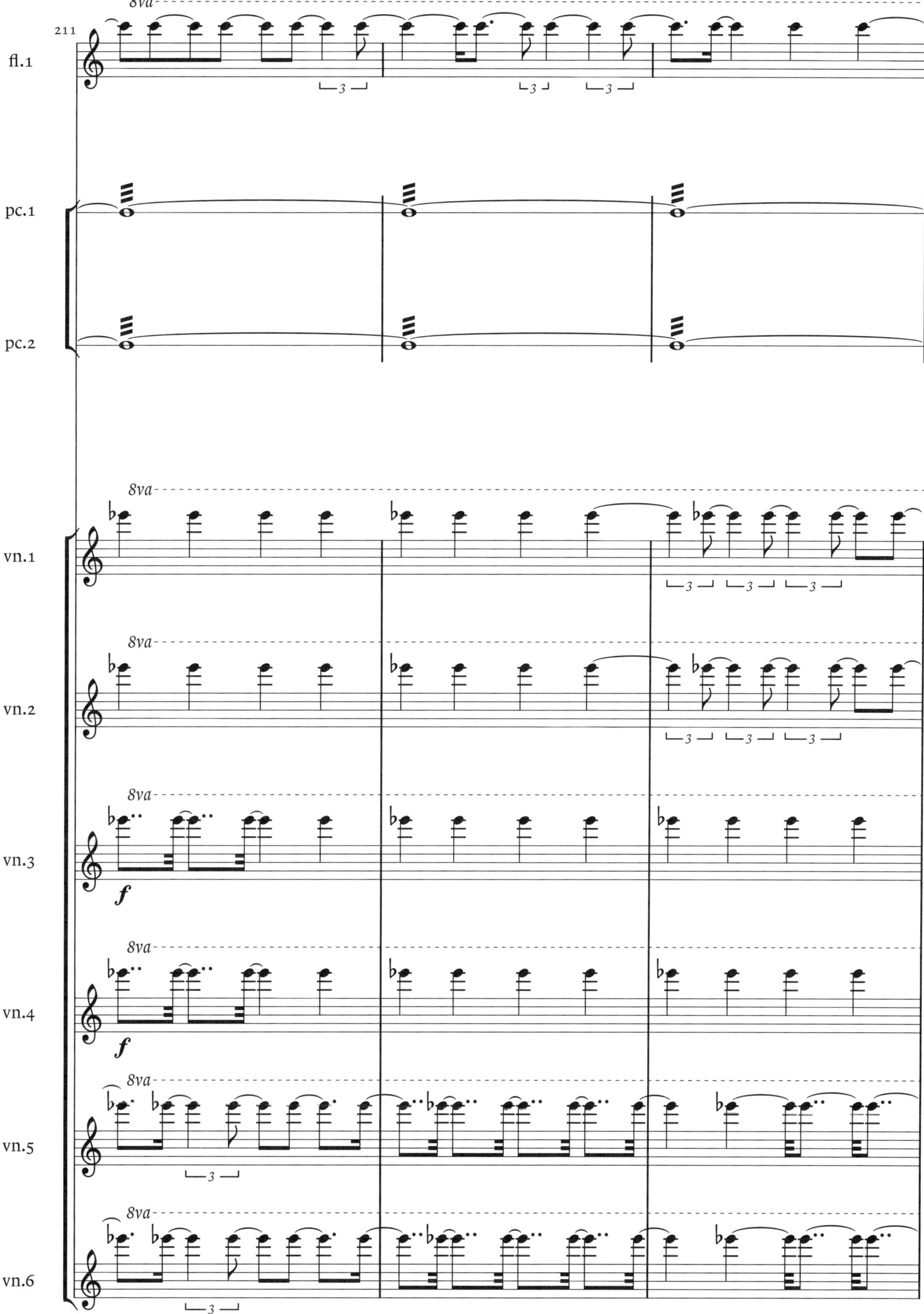
211
fl.1
pc.1
pc.2
vn.1
vn.2
vn.3
vn.4
vn.5
vn.6
8va
3
f

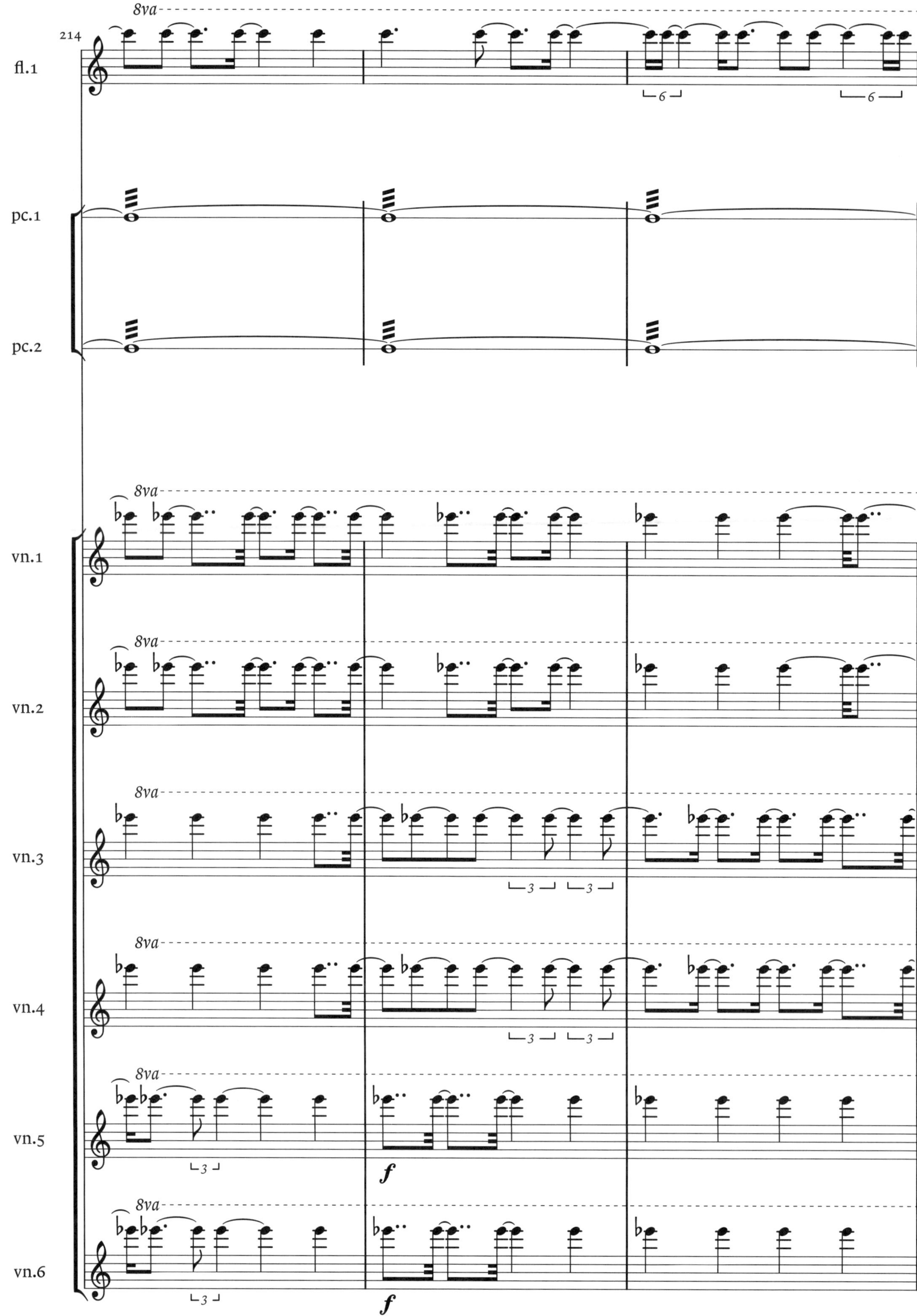
214
8va
fl.1
6
pc.1
pc.2
vn.1
vn.2
vn.3
3
vn.4
vn.5
f
vn.6

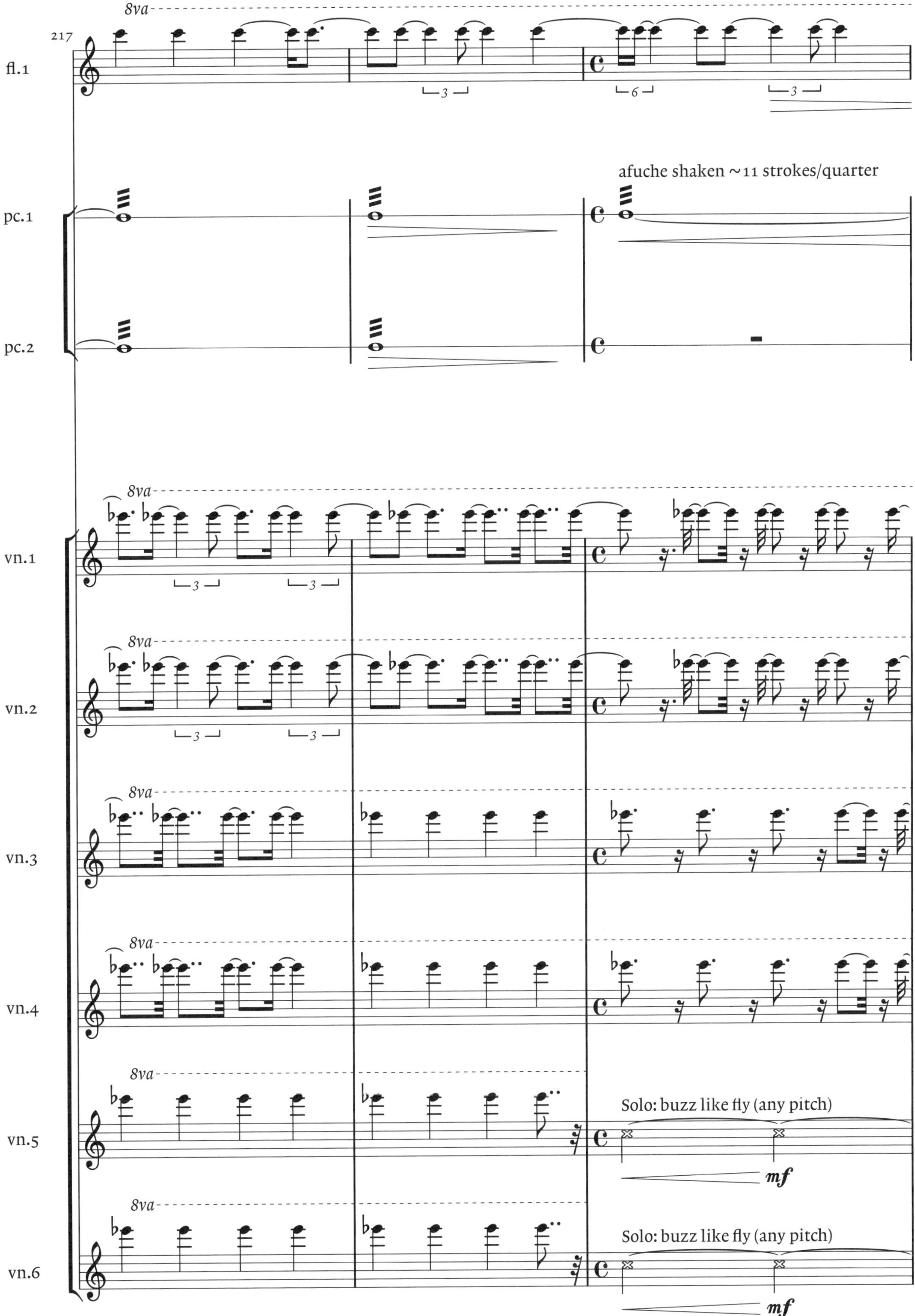
8va
217
fl.1
afuche shaken ~11 strokes/quarter
pc.1
pc.2
8va
vn.1
8va
vn.2
8va
vn.3
8va
vn.4
8va
vn.5
Solo: buzz like fly (any pitch)
mf
8va
vn.6
Solo: buzz like fly (any pitch)
mf

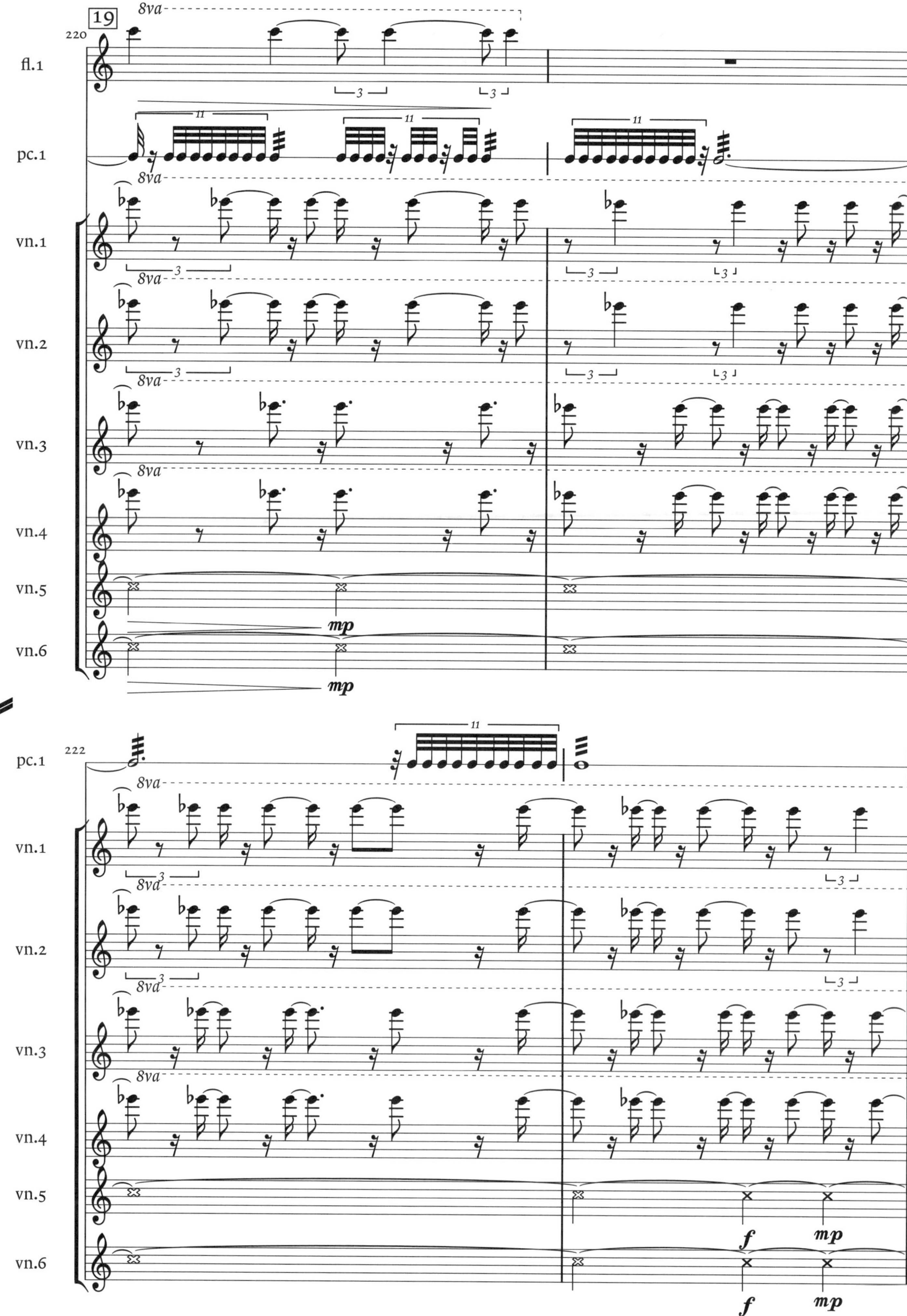
19
220
8va
fl.1
11
pc.1
vn.1
vn.2
vn.3
vn.4
vn.5
vn.6
mp
mp
222
pc.1
vn.1
vn.2
vn.3
vn.4
vn.5
vn.6
f
mp
f
mp

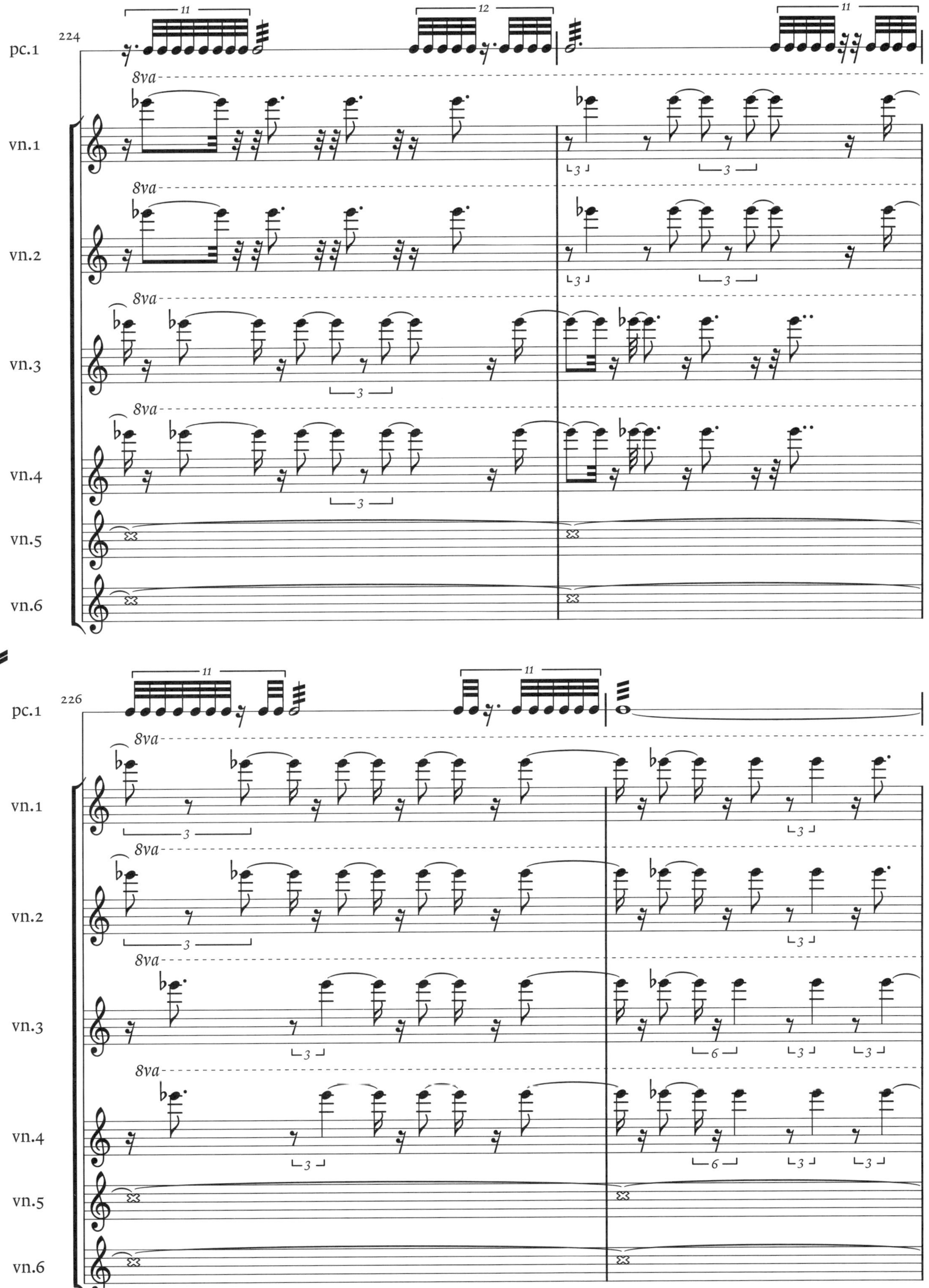
224
pc.1
vn.1
vn.2
vn.3
vn.4
vn.5
vn.6
226
pc.1
vn.1
vn.2
vn.3
vn.4
vn.5
vn.6

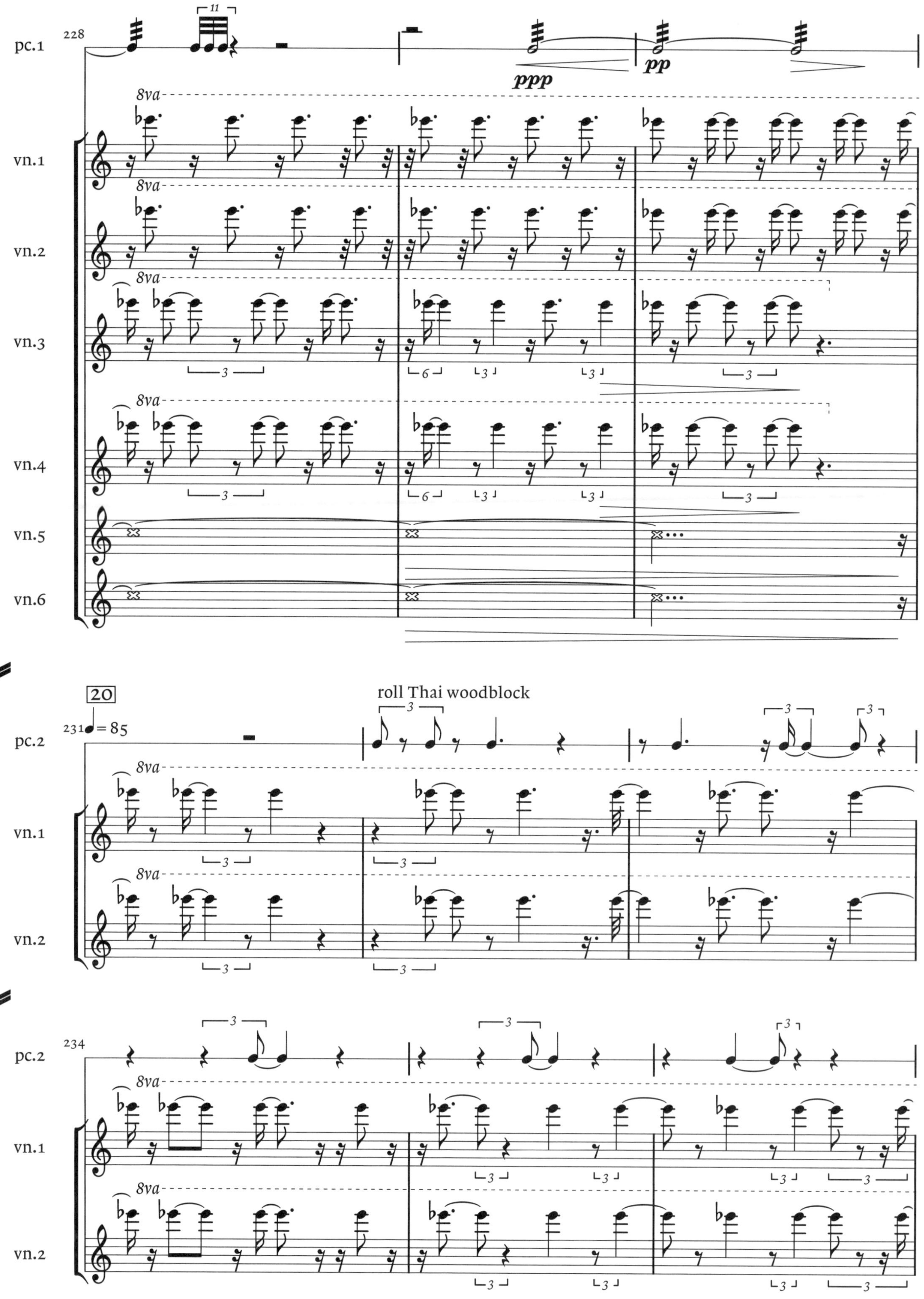
228
pc.1
11
ppp
pp
8va
vn.1
vn.2
vn.3
vn.4
vn.5
vn.6
20
231 ♩= 85
roll Thai woodblock
pc.2
234

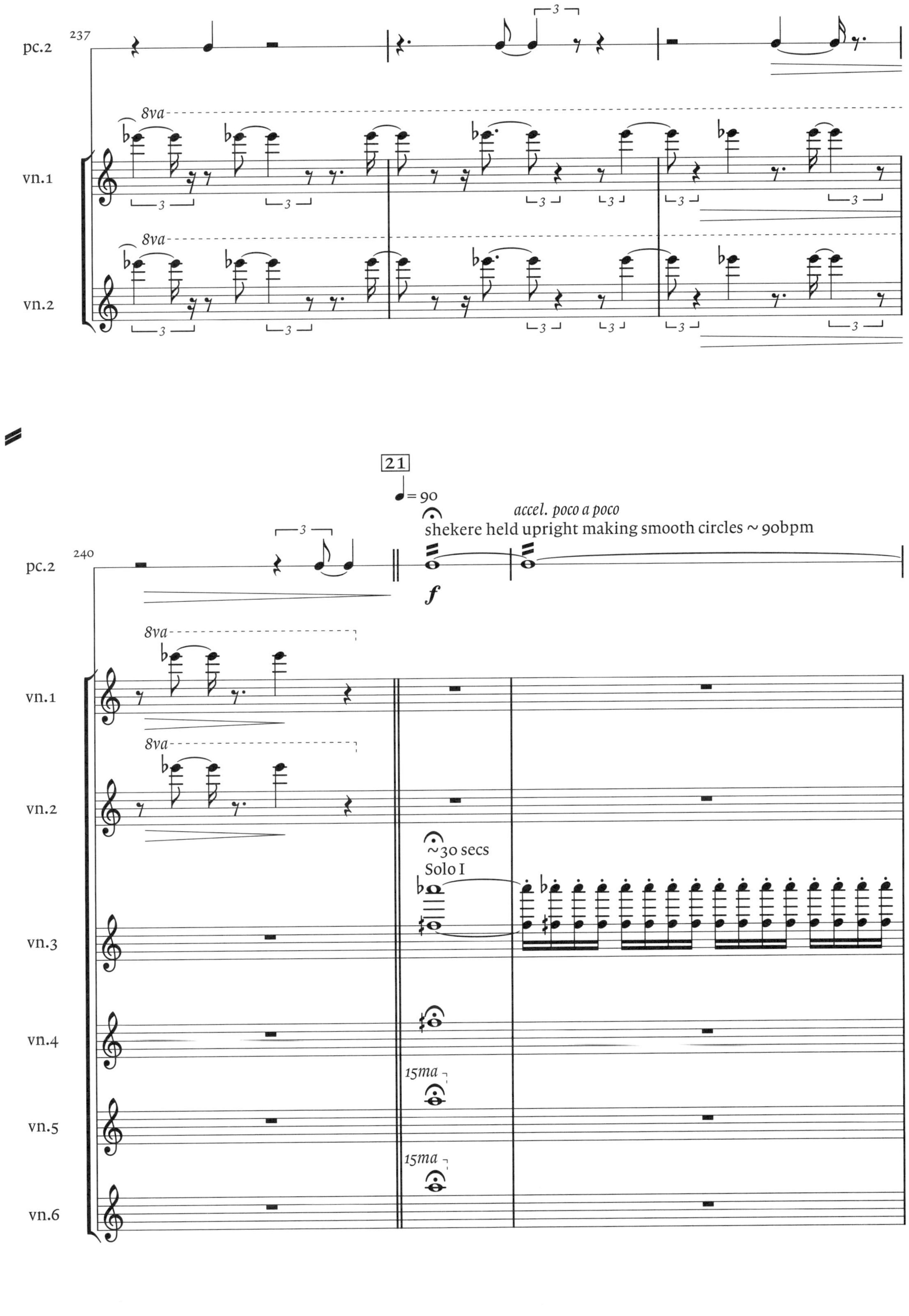

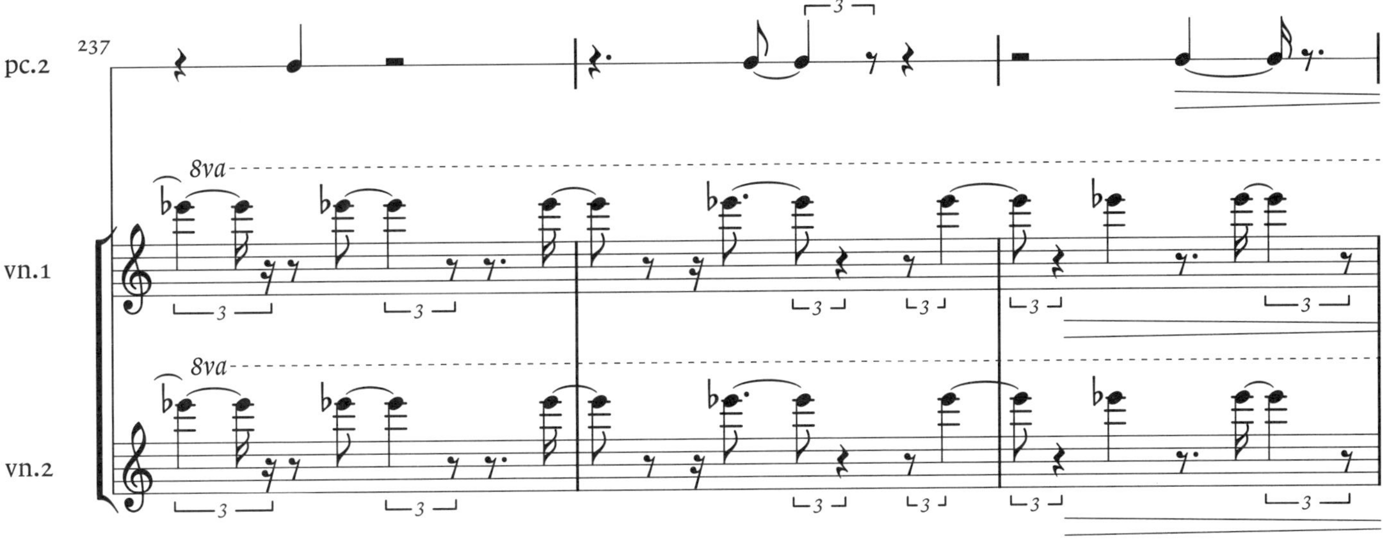

240

pc.2

21

♩= 90

accel. poco a poco

shekere held upright making smooth circles ~ 90bpm

f

vn.1

8va

vn.2

8va

~30 secs

Solo I

vn.3

vn.4

15ma

vn.5

15ma

vn.6

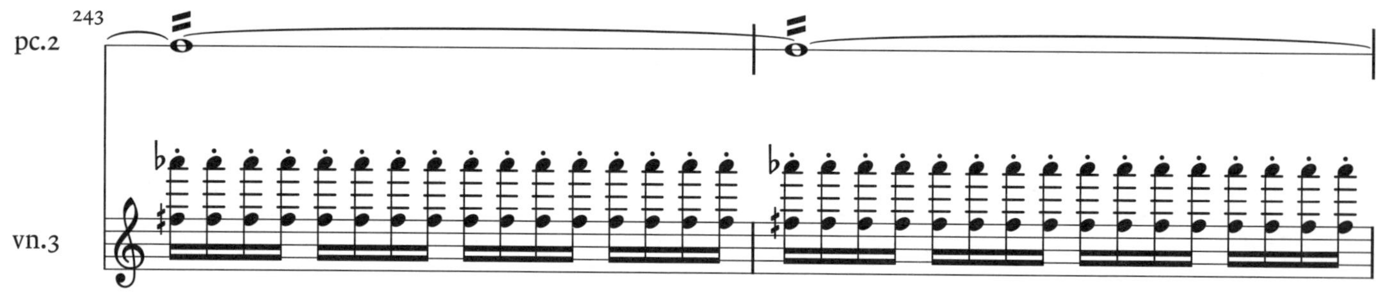
243
pc.2
vn.3

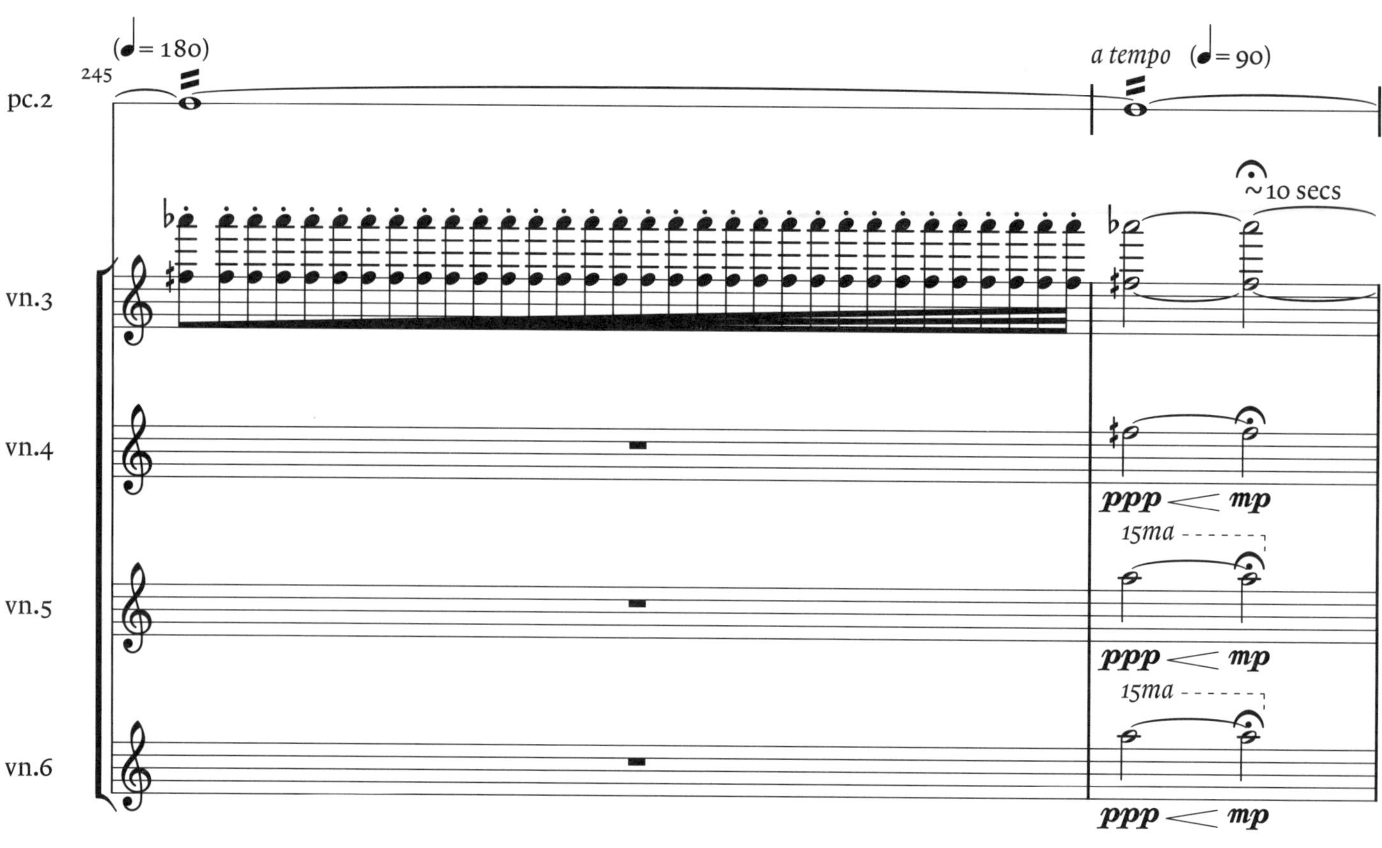
(♩= 180)
245
pc.2
a tempo (♩= 90)
~10 secs
vn.3
vn.4
ppp
mp
15ma
vn.5
ppp
mp
15ma
vn.6
ppp
mp

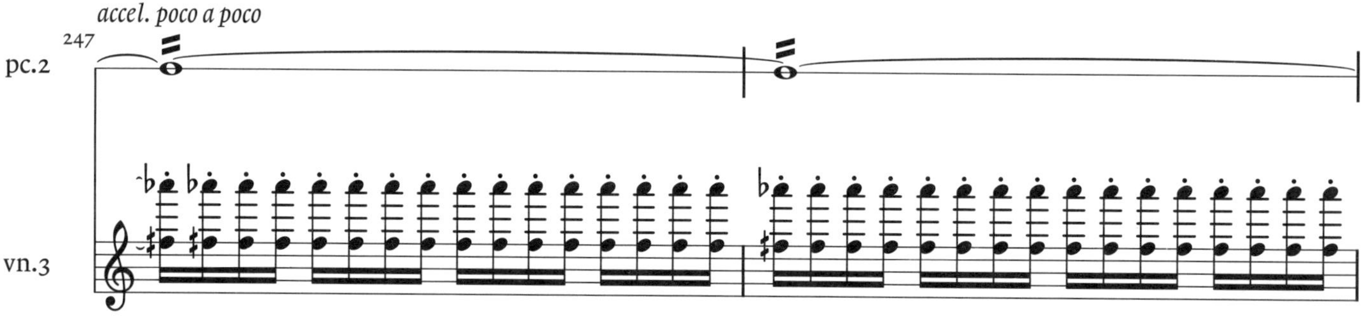
accel. poco a poco
247
pc.2
vn.3

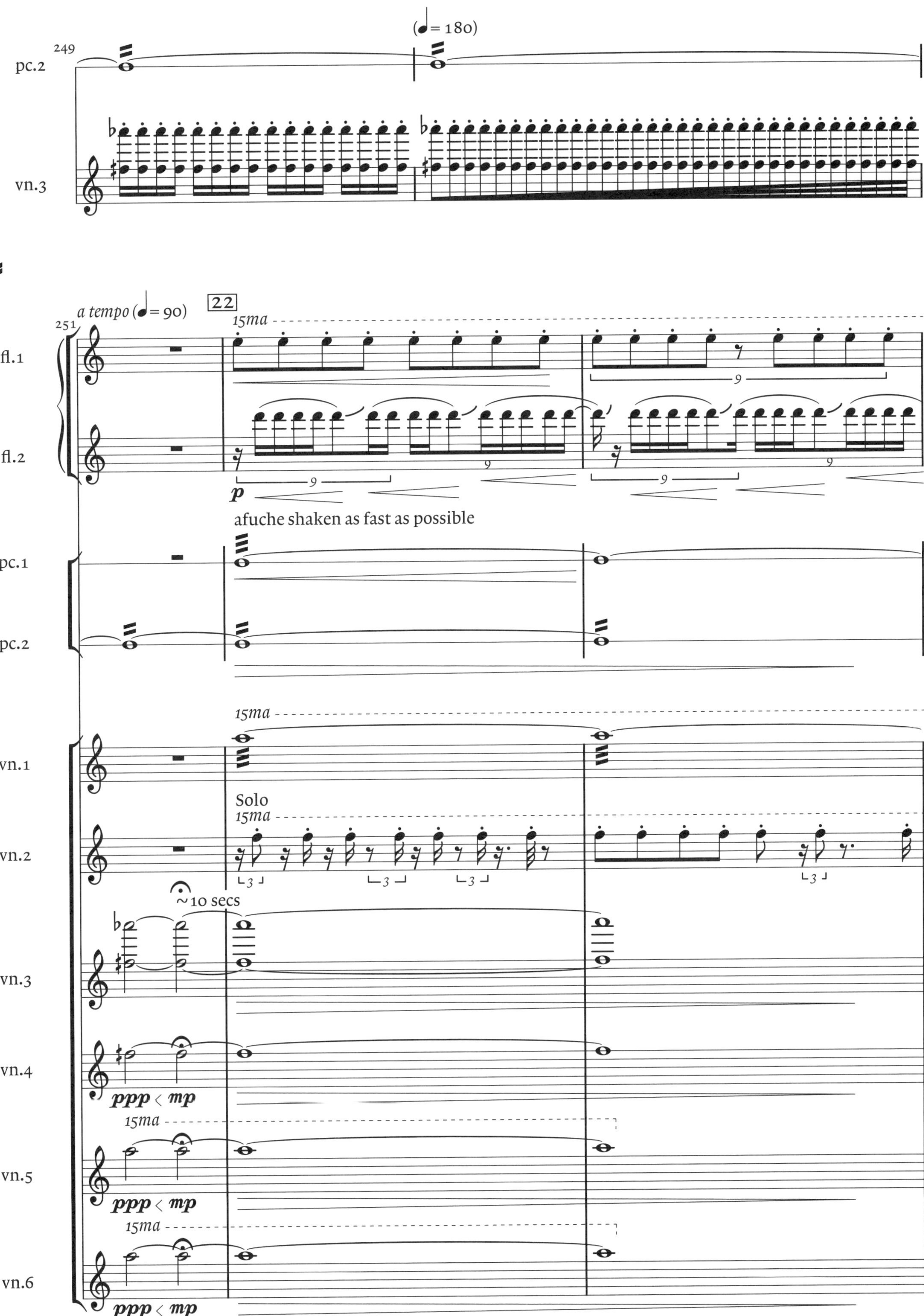

249
pc.2
(♩= 180)
vn.3
a tempo (♩= 90)
22
251
fl.1
15ma
9
fl.2
9
9
9
9
p
afuche shaken as fast as possible
pc.1
pc.2
15ma
vn.1
Solo
15ma
vn.2
3
3
3
3
~10 secs
vn.3
vn.4
ppp < mp
15ma
vn.5
ppp < mp
15ma
vn.6
ppp < mp

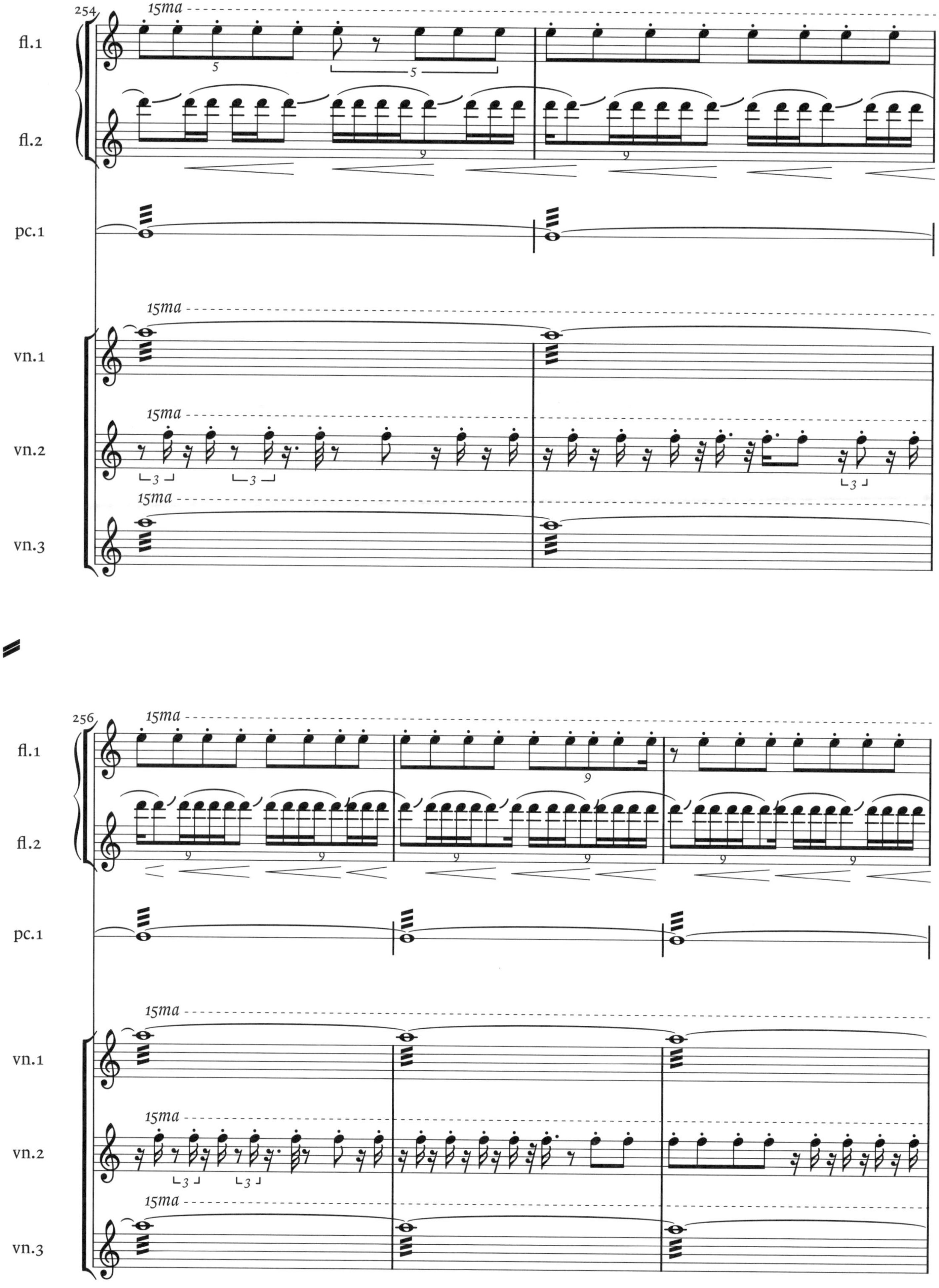

254

fl.1

fl.2

pc.1

vn.1

vn.2

vn.3

15ma

5

9

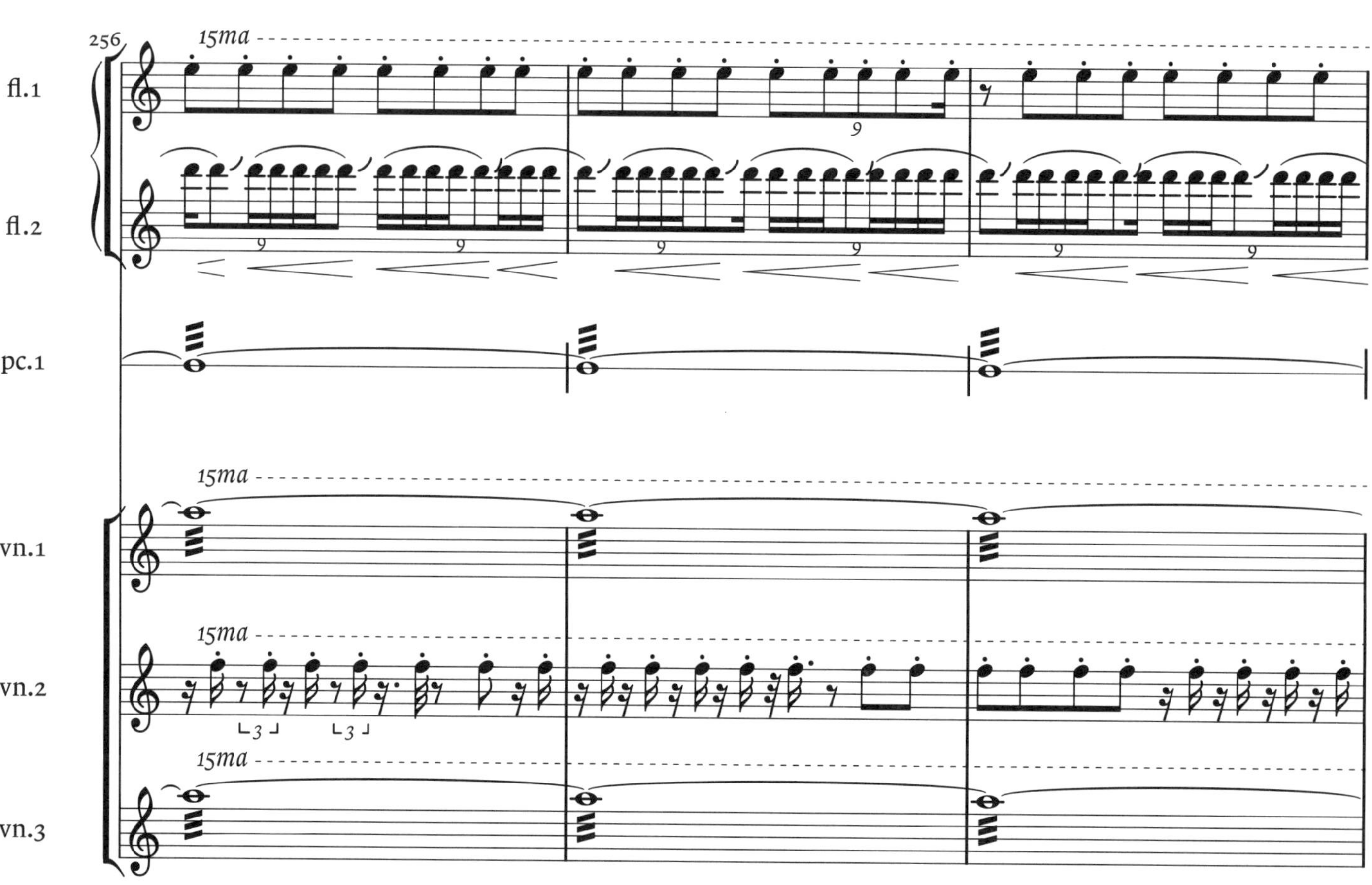

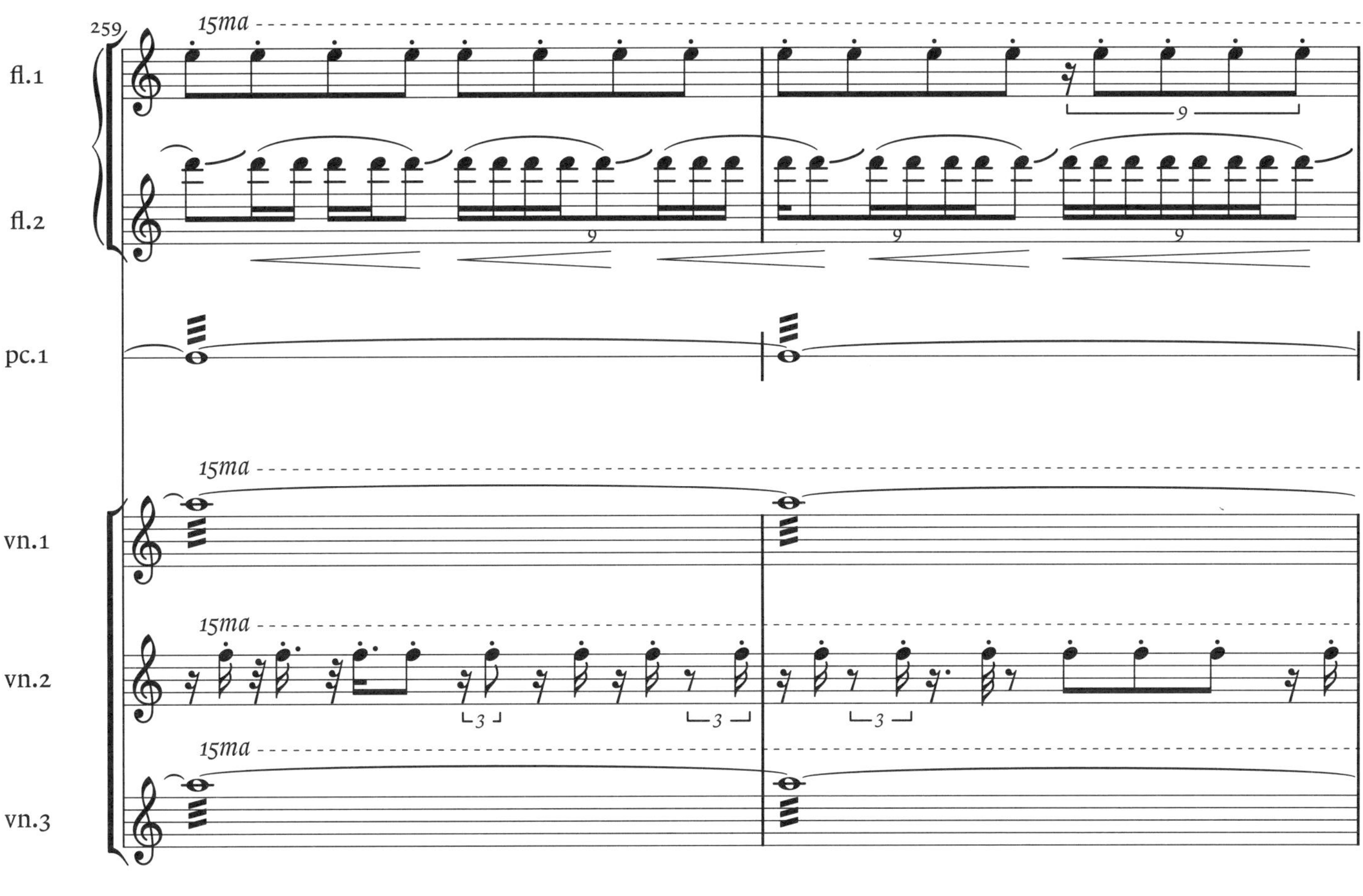
259
fl.1
fl.2
pc.1
vn.1
vn.2
vn.3
15ma
9
3

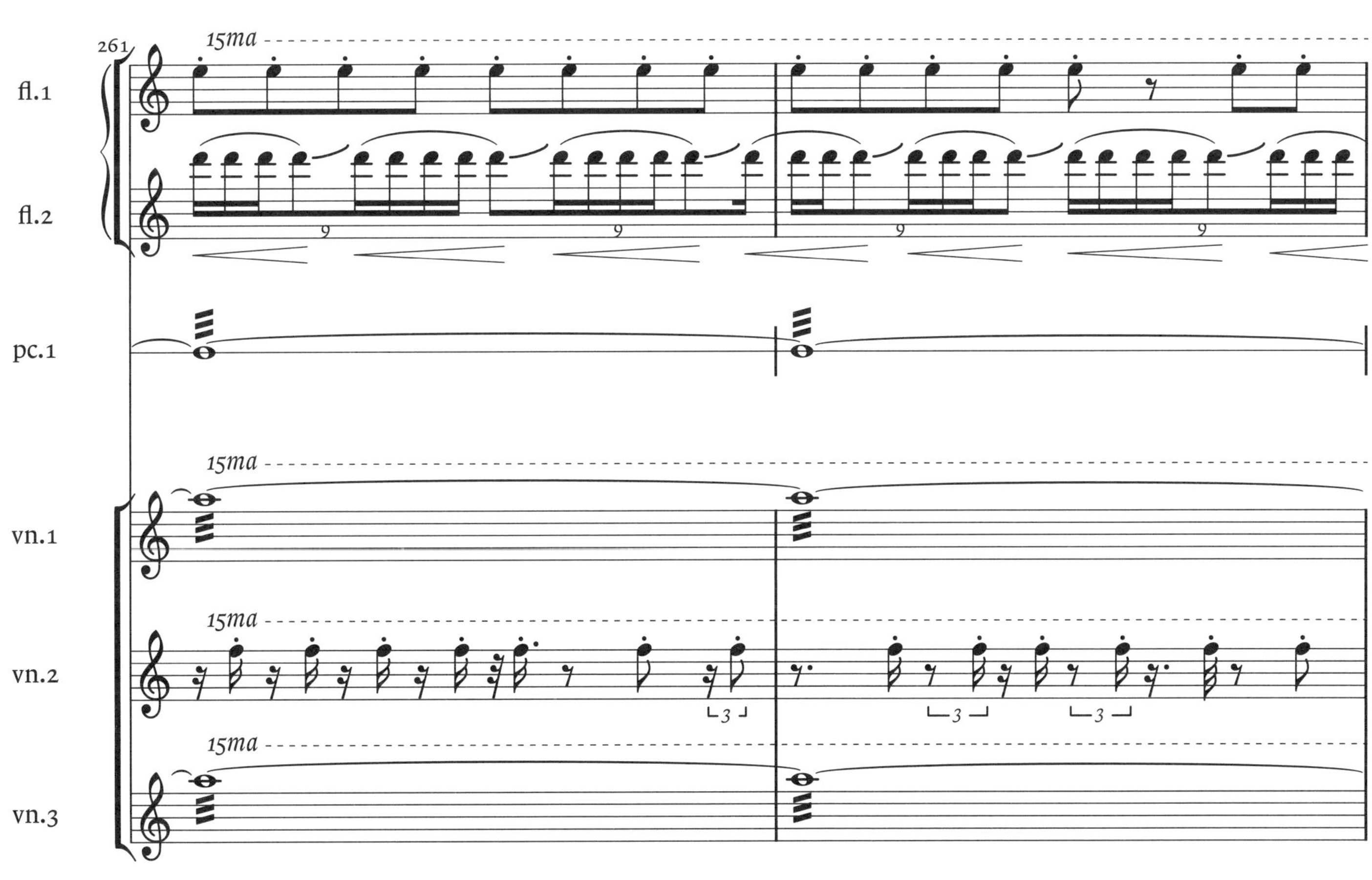
261
fl.1
fl.2
pc.1
vn.1
vn.2
vn.3
15ma
9
3

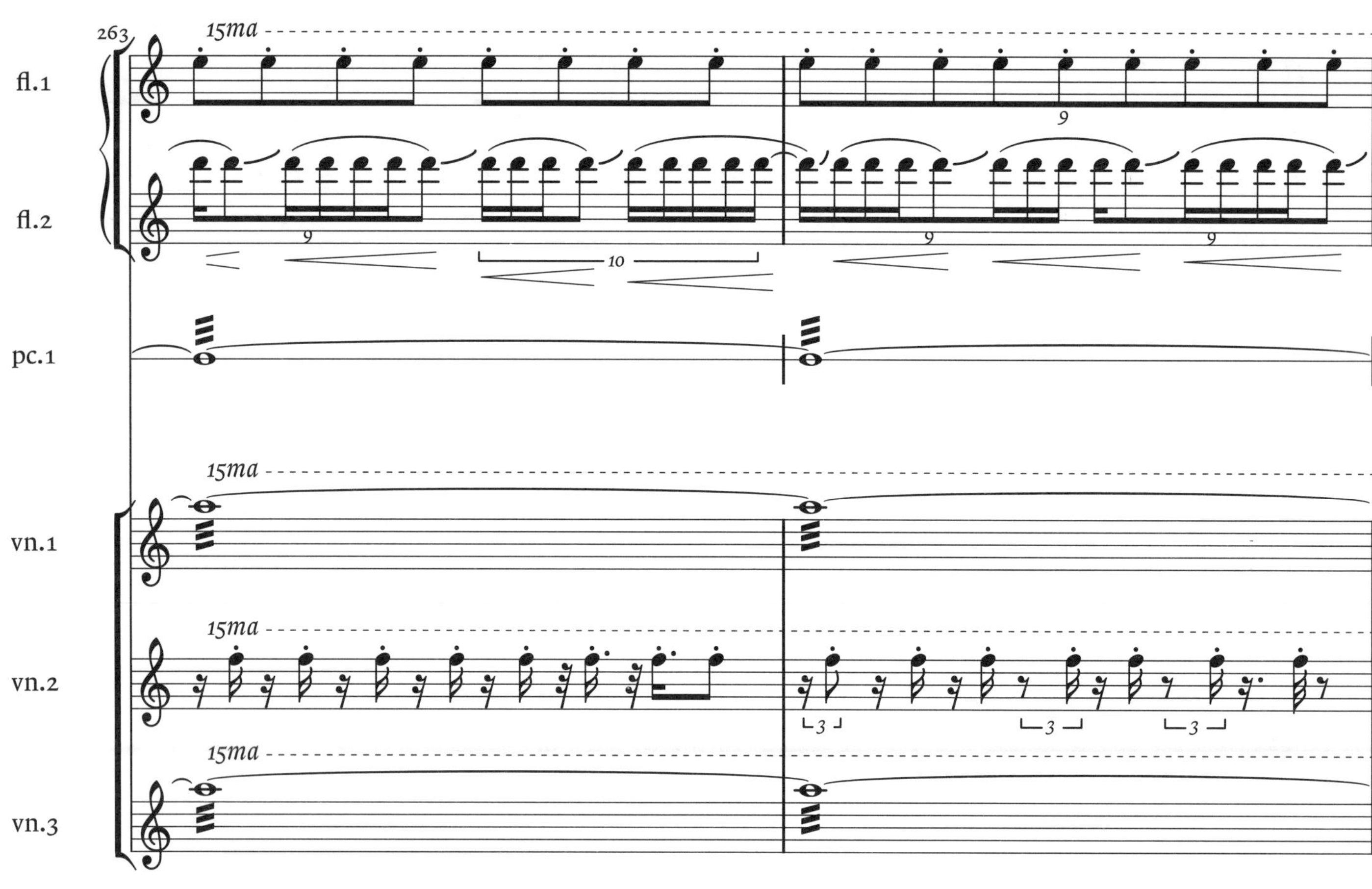
263
fl.1
fl.2
pc.1
vn.1
vn.2
vn.3
15ma
9
10
3

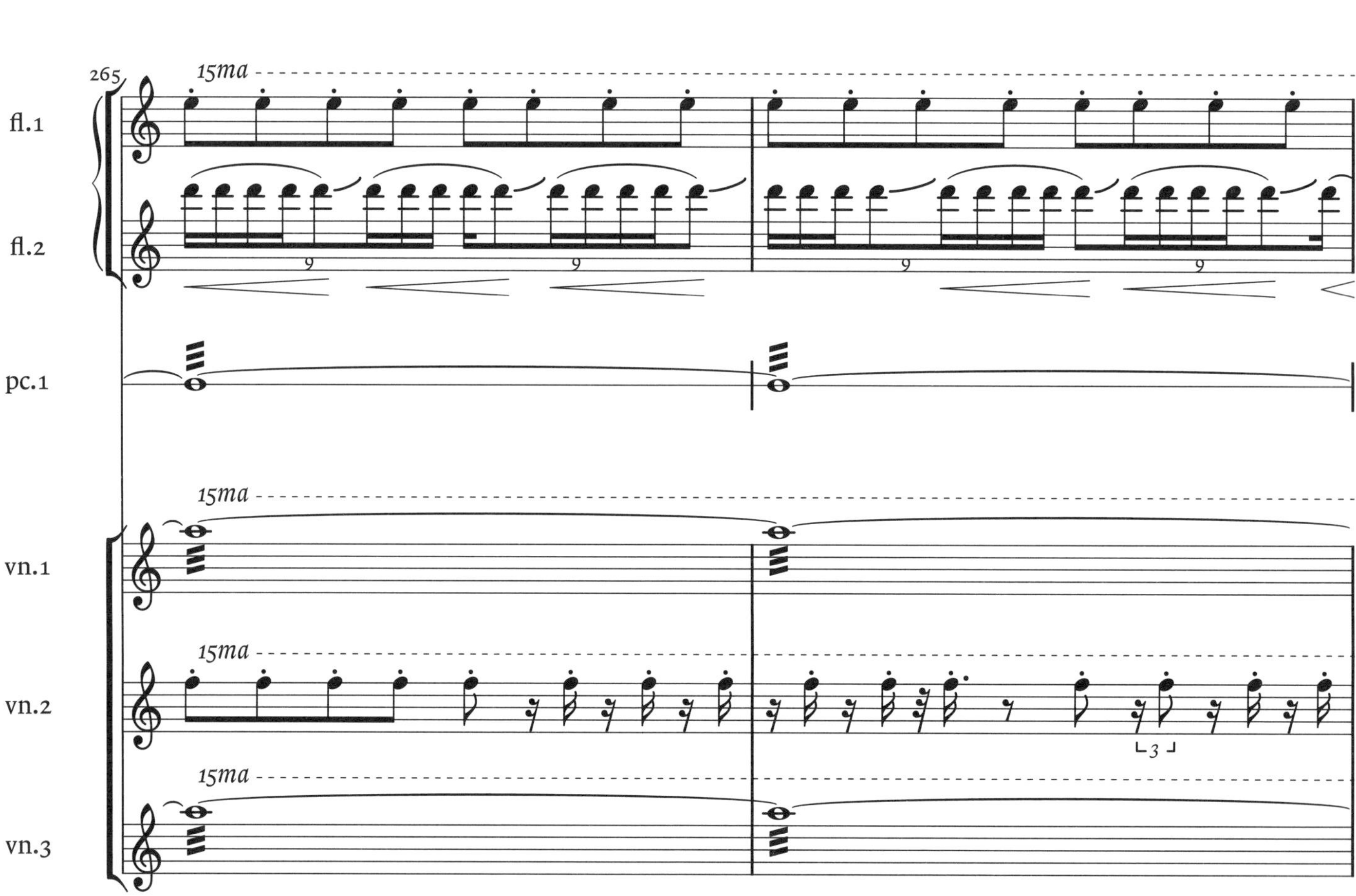
265
fl.1
fl.2
pc.1
vn.1
vn.2
vn.3
15ma
9
3

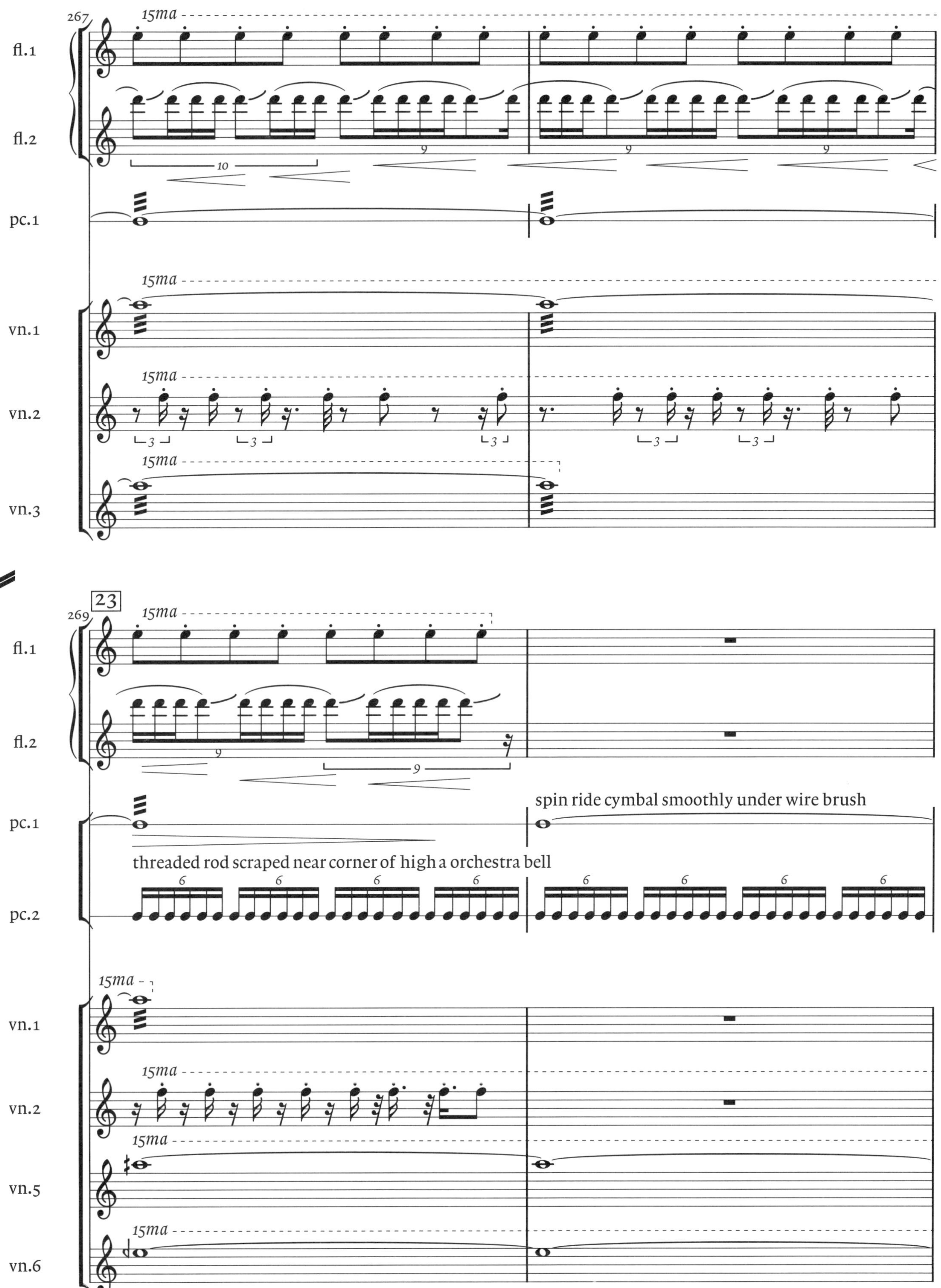
267
fl.1
fl.2
pc.1
vn.1
vn.2
vn.3
15ma
23
269
pc.2
vn.5
vn.6
spin ride cymbal smoothly under wire brush
threaded rod scraped near corner of high a orchestra bell

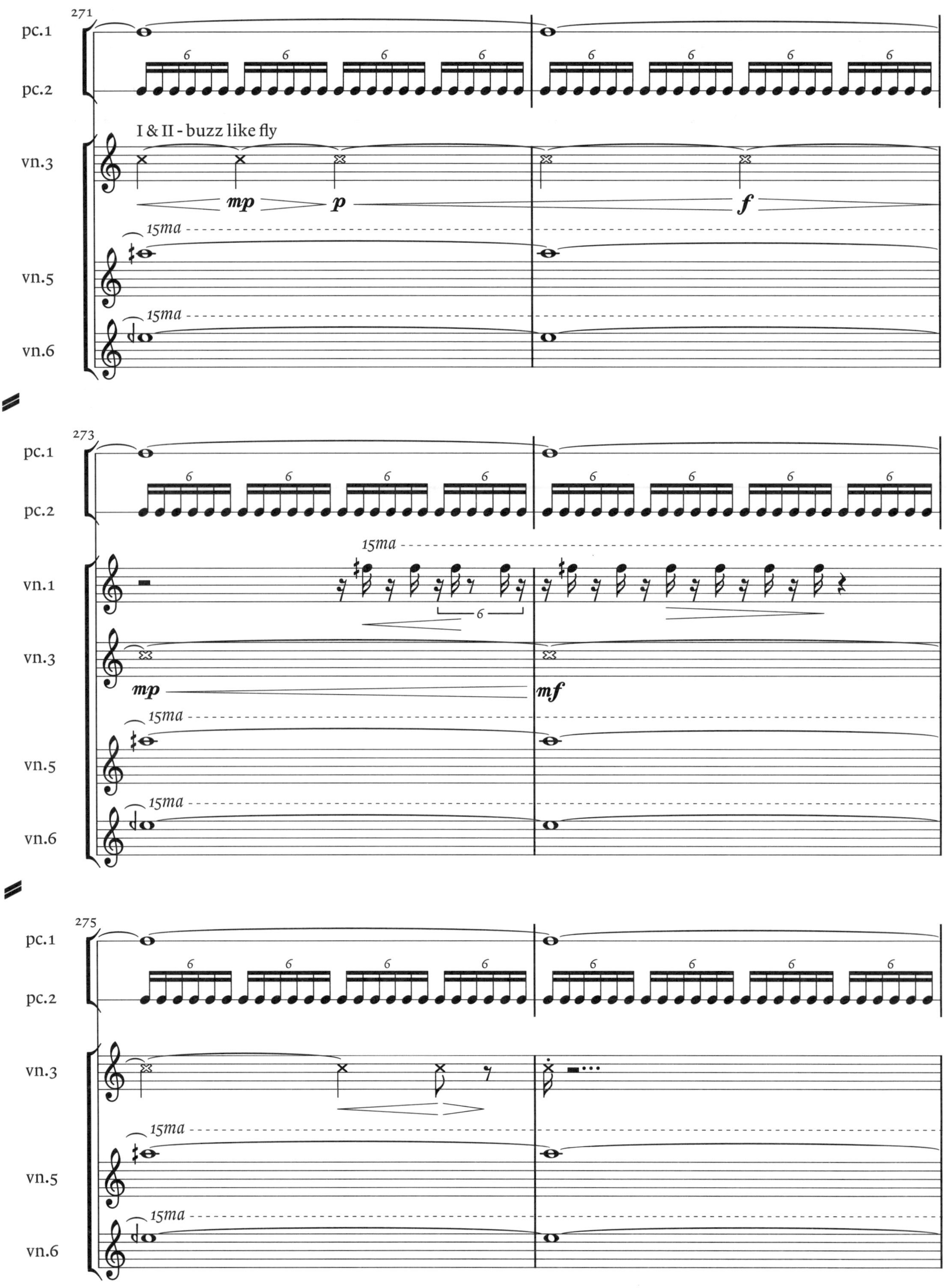
271
pc.1
pc.2
I & II - buzz like fly
vn.3
mp
p
f
15ma
vn.5
vn.6
273
vn.1
mp
mf
275

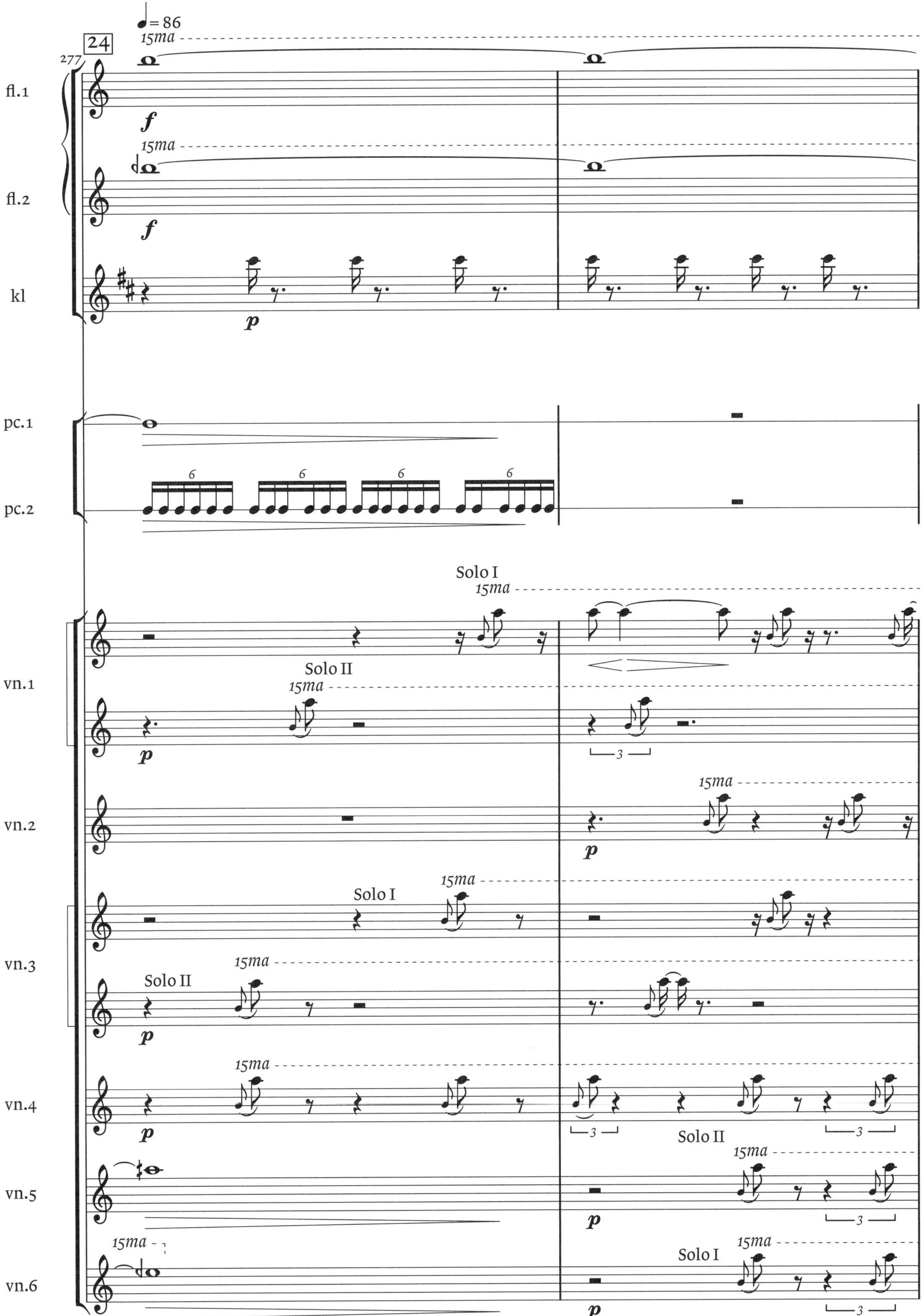

24
277
♩= 86
15ma
fl.1
fl.2
kl
pc.1
pc.2
vn.1
vn.2
vn.3
vn.4
vn.5
vn.6
Solo I
Solo II

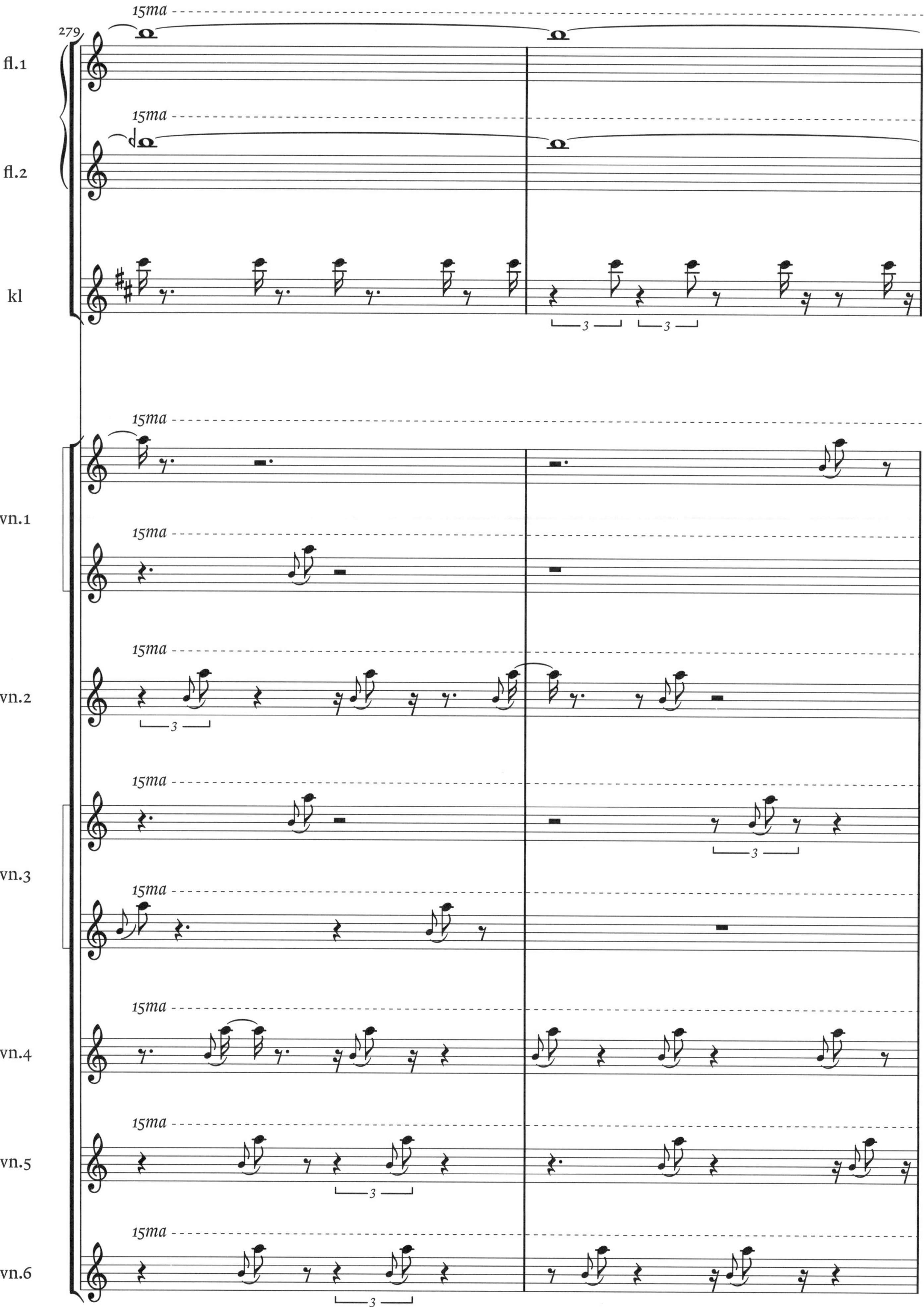
279
15ma
fl.1
fl.2
kl
3
vn.1
vn.2
vn.3
vn.4
vn.5
vn.6

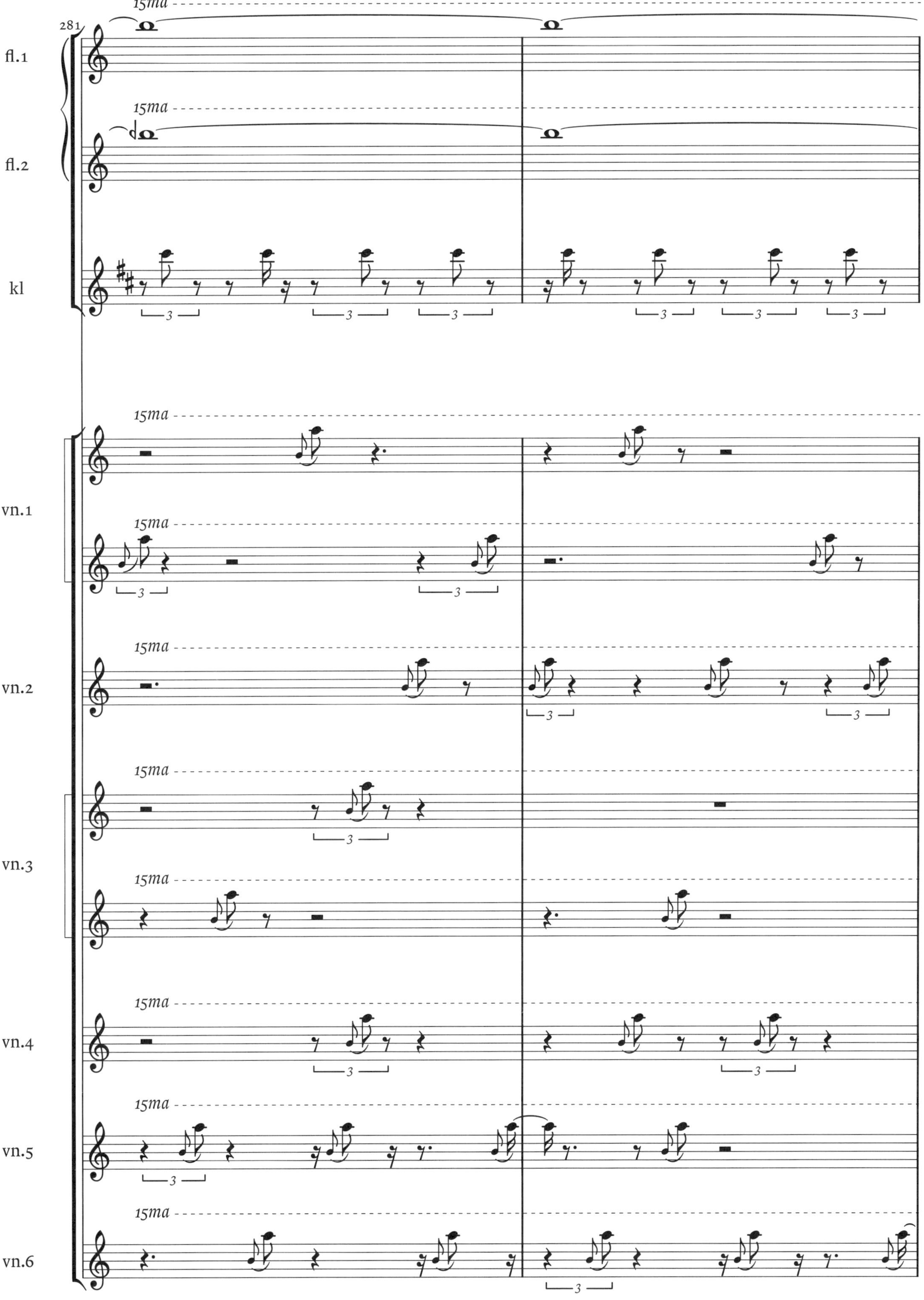
281
fl.1
fl.2
kl
vn.1
vn.2
vn.3
vn.4
vn.5
vn.6
15ma

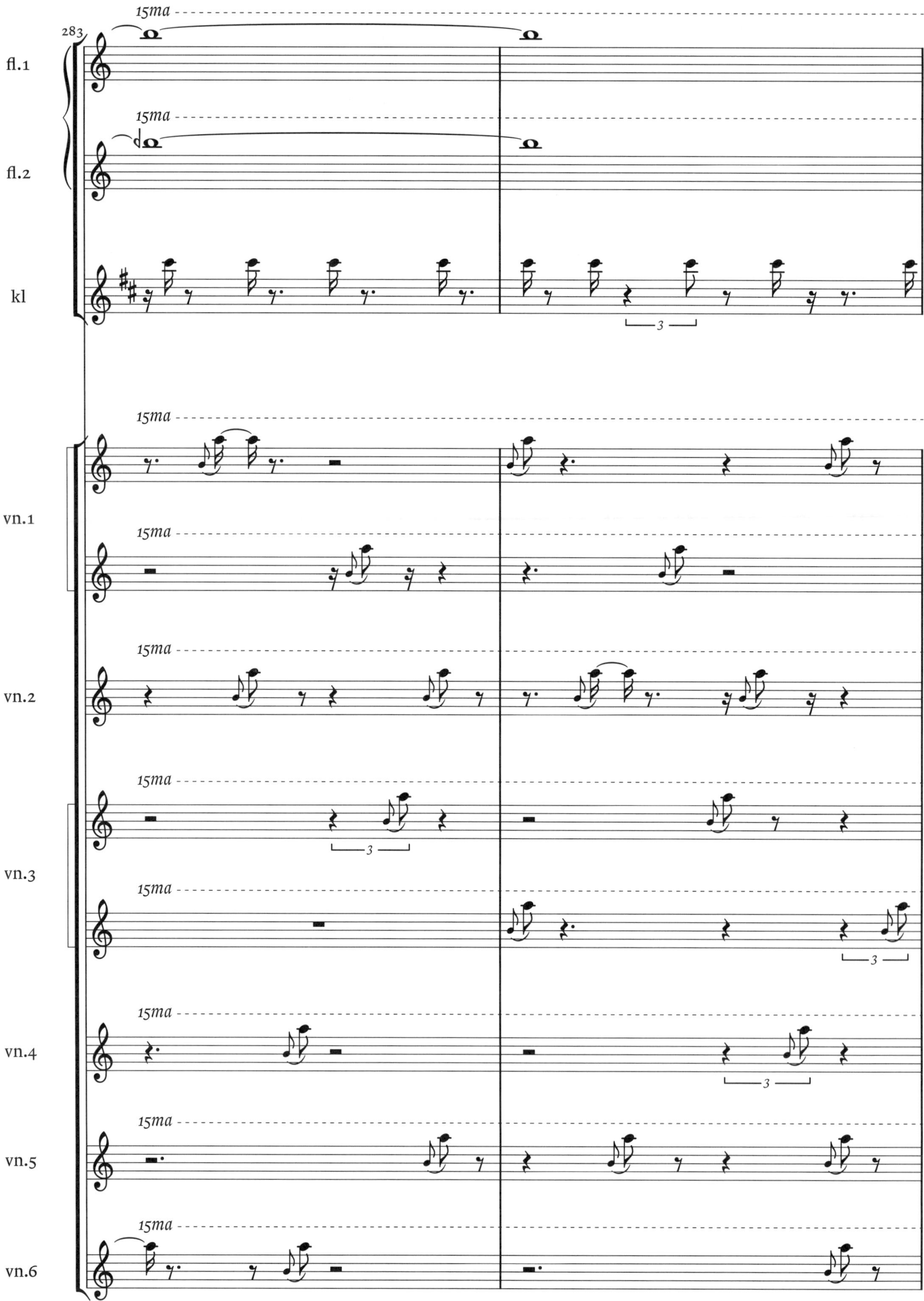
283
fl.1
fl.2
kl
vn.1
vn.2
vn.3
vn.4
vn.5
vn.6
15ma
3

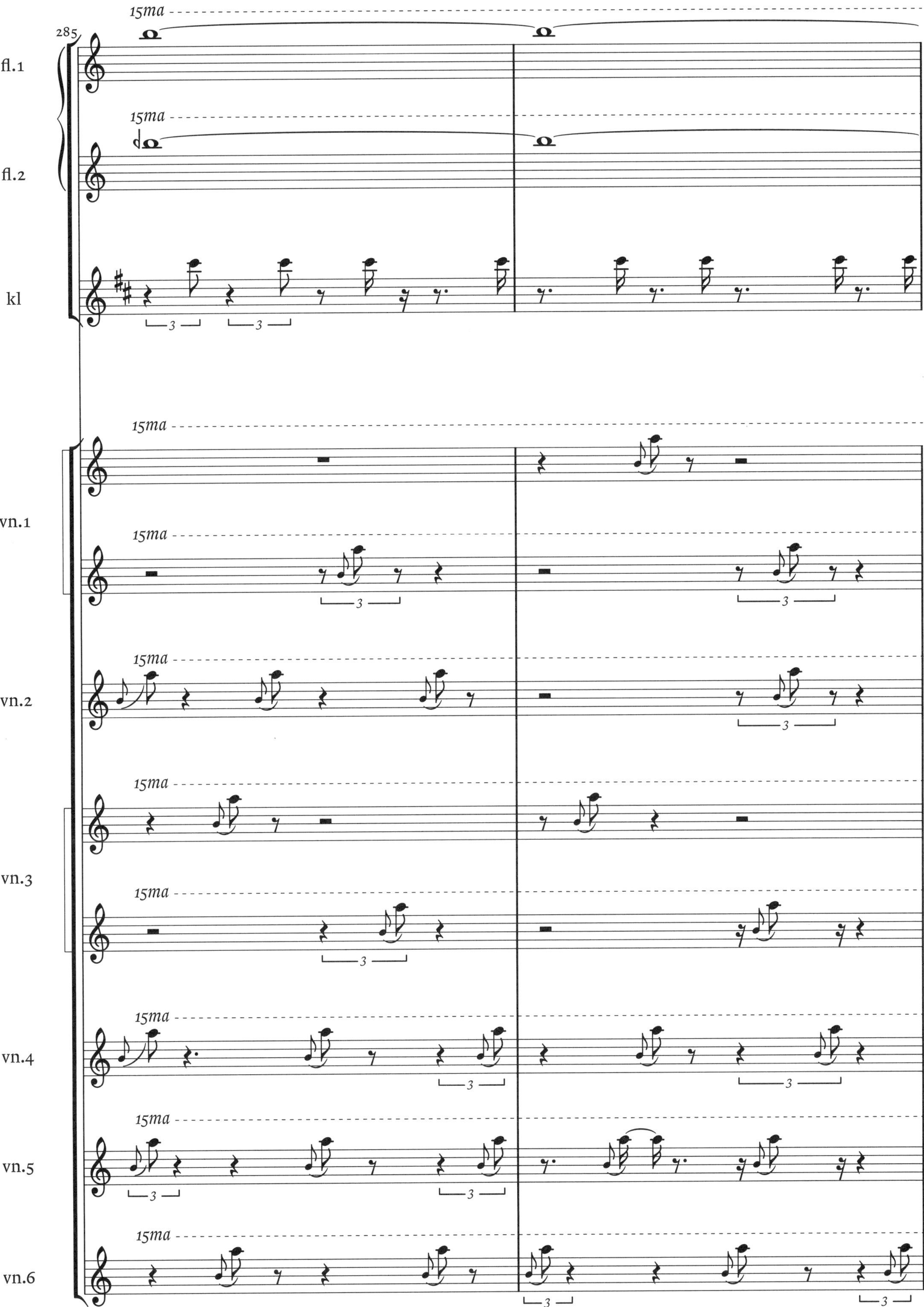
285
fl.1
fl.2
kl
vn.1
vn.2
vn.3
vn.4
vn.5
vn.6
15ma

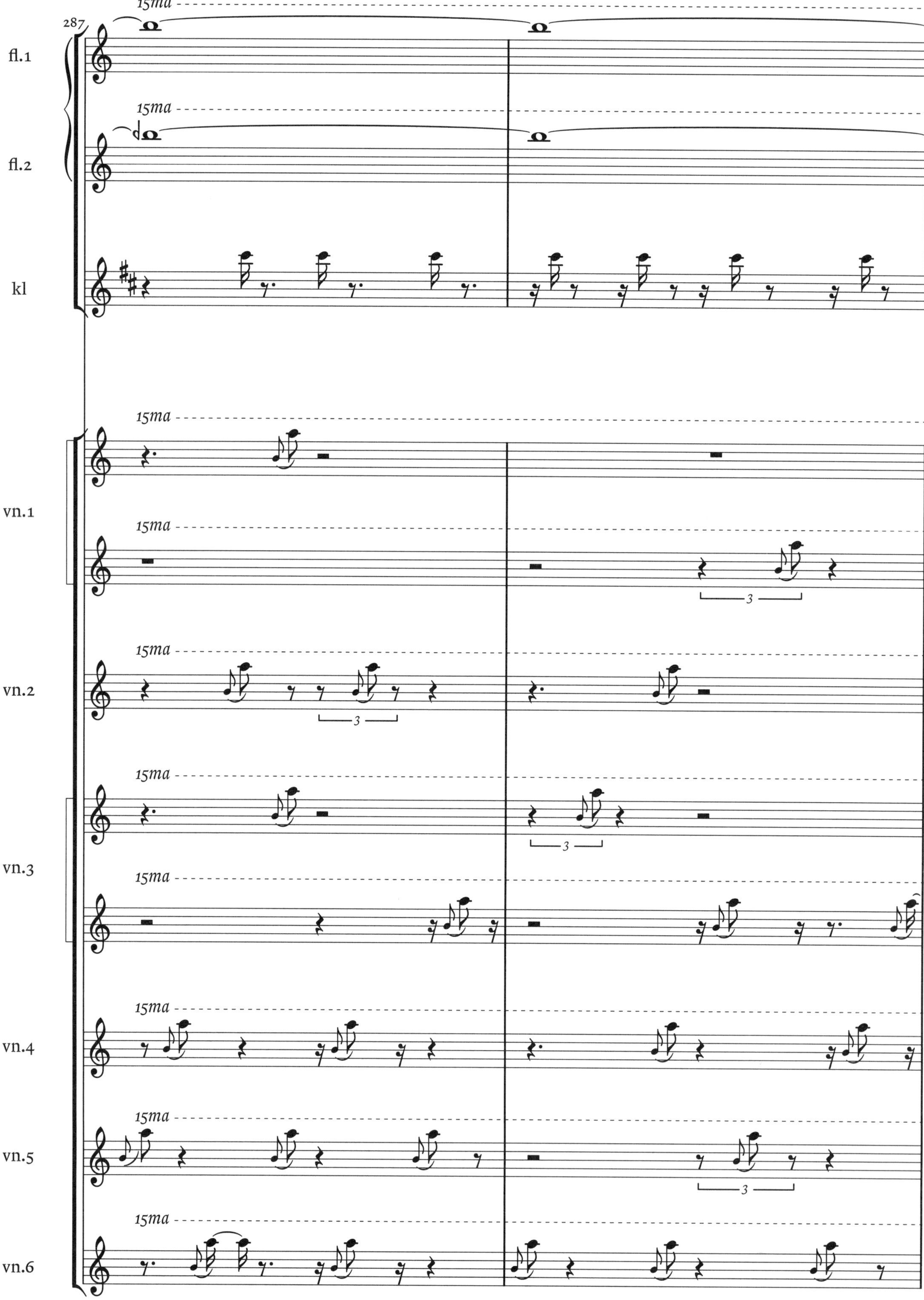
287
15ma
fl.1
fl.2
kl
vn.1
vn.2
vn.3
vn.4
vn.5
vn.6
3

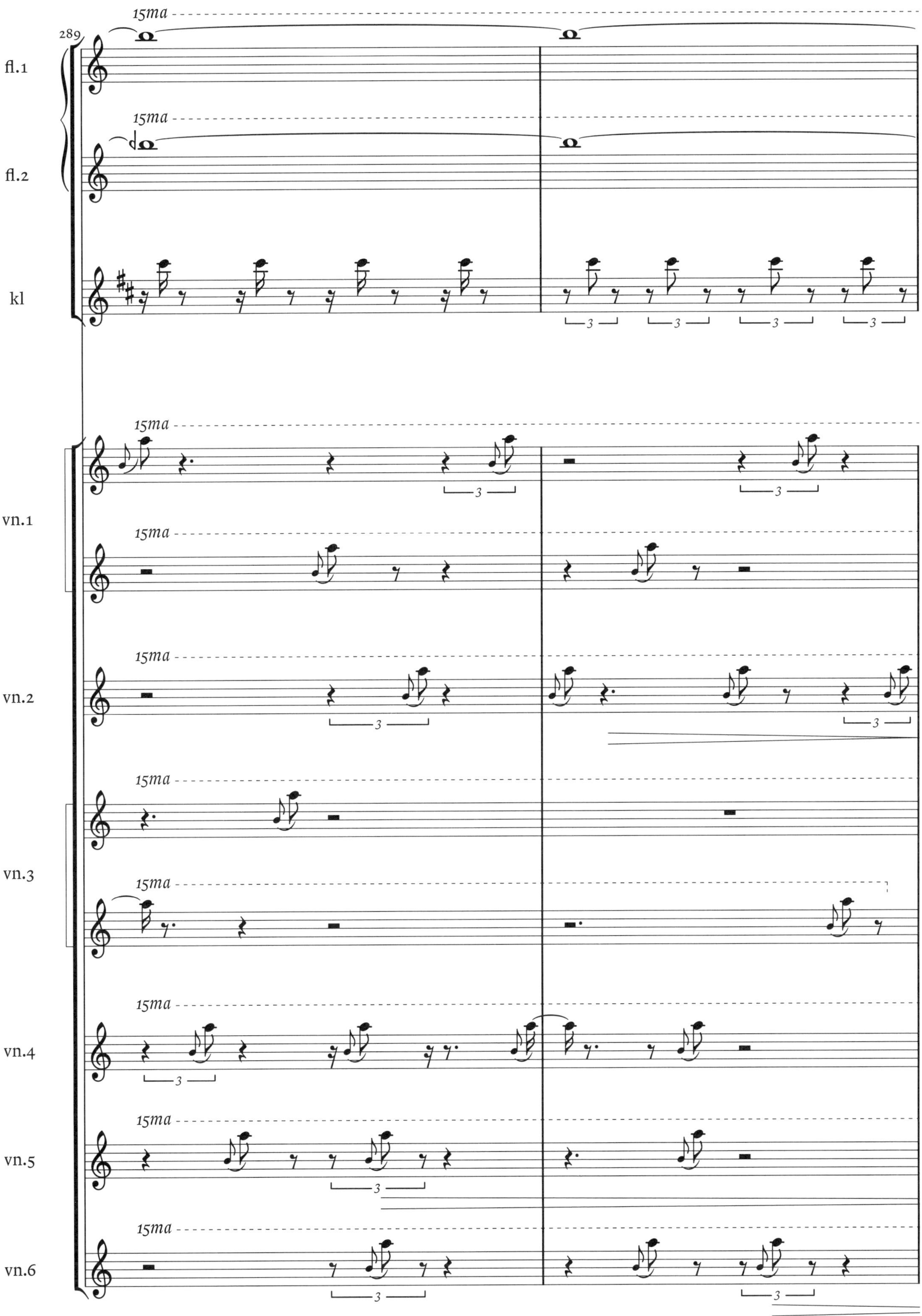
289
fl.1
fl.2
kl
vn.1
vn.2
vn.3
vn.4
vn.5
vn.6
15ma
3

25

291

15ma
fl.1
15ma
fl.2
kl
cut air with wire brush
pc.1
mf
mp
15ma
vn.1
15ma
p
15ma
vn.2
p
15ma
vn.3
3
p
15ma
vn.4
p
15ma
vn.5
3
p
15ma
vn.6
p

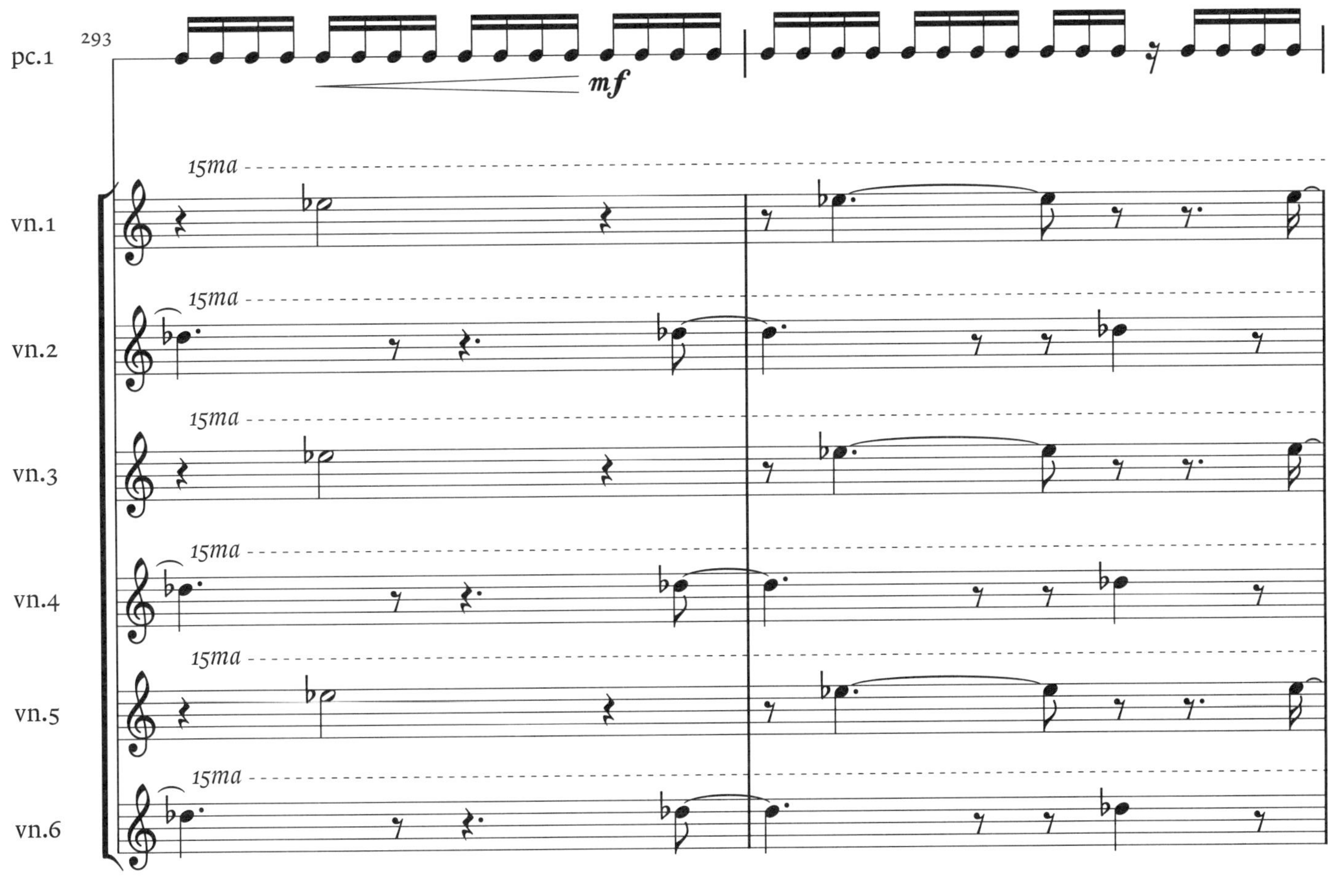

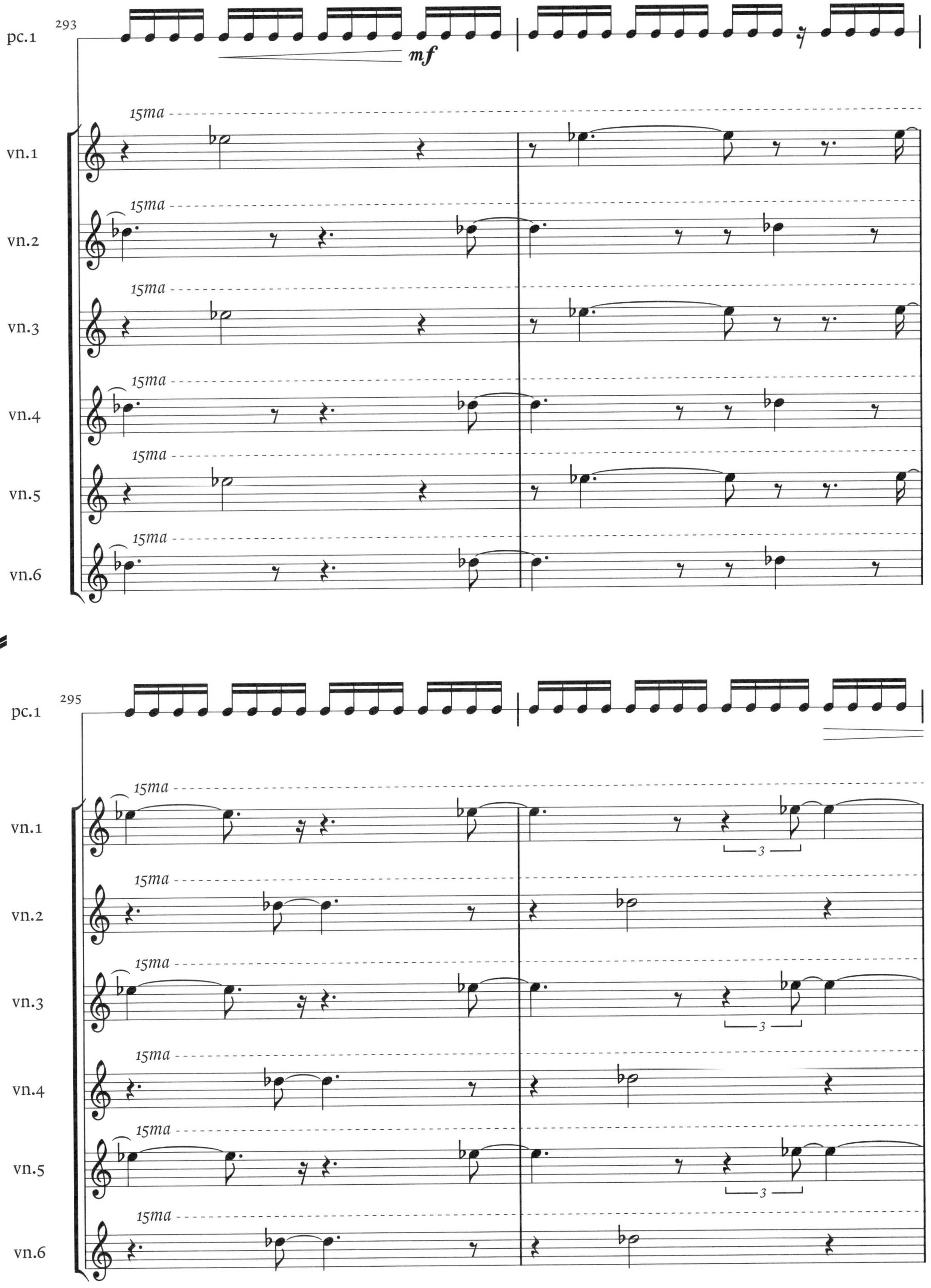

295
pc.1
15ma
vn.1
vn.2
vn.3
vn.4
vn.5
vn.6
3

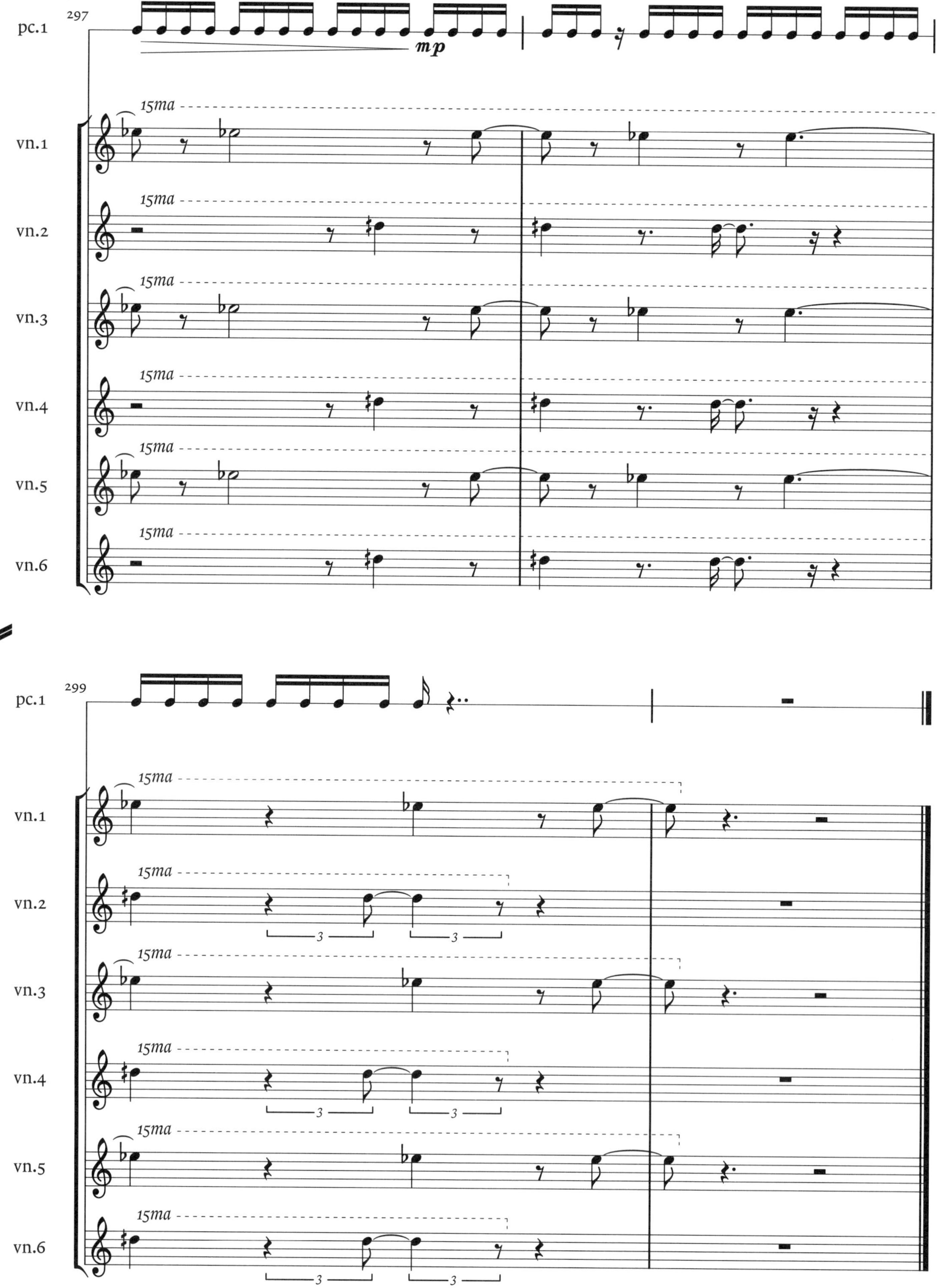
297
pc.1
mp
15ma
vn.1
vn.2
vn.3
vn.4
vn.5
vn.6
299
3

Clarinet

Flute *Flute*

Percussion 1 *Percussion 2*

Violin 4 *Violin 4*

Violin 2 *Violin 2* *Violin 6* *Violin 6*

Violin 3 *Violin 3*

Violin 1 *Violin 1* *Violin 5* *Violin 5*

Conductor

Performance Notes

Performers should bear in mind that for a cricket, every utterance is "one"–each chirp is complete, not felt as part of a phrase. Soloists should take care to deliver repeated notes with the same technique; bowing in the same direction where practical, for example. In some of the sections, for instance numbers *2* and *8*, there are two players chirping alike but at different dynamics. What is being represented here is a difference in distance from an imaginary microphone rather than a difference in intensity. Mood and technique vary no more between crickets than between chirps.

By and large, conventional expressive musical sounds are to be avoided. Violins and flutes should play *senza vibrato* except when explicitly instructed.

In some vignettes a single soloist may chirp in the foreground while the distant multitude of his fellows is represented by a cluster in the violins. Bearing that in mind, care can be taken to be sure that the tone of that portion of the cluster is appropriate. When the accompanying cluster includes pitches far from that of the soloists, these are likely produced by other insects: in those cases some difference in tone may be welcome.

In the recordings that are the basis of this work sections are generally cross-faded from one to the next. Bear this in mind when transitioning between sections: long initial *crescendi* should be *da niente*, technique permitting, and final *decrescendi* likewise. These may also be extended if convenient.

One sound that should be scrupulously avoided is the sound of strings tuning within a section. If it is absolutely necessary to adjust, try to do so between notes, or simply forge ahead in a kind of *ad hoc* cluster; either is preferable to hearing a pitch sliding.

When orchestra bell keys are rasped by threaded rods or rhythm sticks they should be held pinched on or resting on their nodes so that they ring as well as possible. When the shakers and maracas are shaken or brushed, or the ride cymbal spun, care should be taken to minimize any impression of pulsation: these are meant to be constant environmental noises.

Finally, as regards rhythm, there are few coincidences between lines, and little significance to these. Beyond that, the rhythmic relationships, excepting the percussion duet, are not precious–take care, even when the counting is thorny, to remain, if not serene, let's say matter-of-fact.

Michael Webster
Los Angeles, 2013

Acknowledgements

Thanks to Cecilia Alemani, Crystal Alforque, Brody Albert, Edvard Baratyan, Alessandra Barrett, Jordan Benke, Lionel Bovier, Grace Bowen, Rod Bradley, Ezra Buchla, Paul Calderon, Daniel Cantagallo, Renata Catambas, Benny Chan, Caroline Chin, Tom Chiu, Eric KM Clark, Matthew Cook, Joe Day, Nina Hachigian Day, Keats Diffenbach, Corey Fogel, Pala Garcia, Carissa Gibson, Benjamin Goldenstein, Blanca Gonzalez, Lisa Grzanka, Jessica Han, Orin Hildestad, James Honaker, Robert Johnstone, Christoph Keller, Cindy Kendall, Lauri Firstenberg, Stina Haroldsdottir, Thomai Hatsios, Sarah Hodges, Amanda Hunt, Maria Im, Heather Lockie, Gregory Maldonado, Emanouil Manolov, Richard Massey, Adriana Molello, Aram Moshayedi, Esther Noh, Dimitry Olevsky, Courtney Orlando, Ben Phelps, Monique Prieto, Jean C. Roché, Danielle Roderick, Heber Rodriguez, Albert Romero, Jessica Schmitz, Matthew Schum, Chihiro Shibayama, Stephanie Smith, Alex Sramek, Andy Stanojevich, Mary Jo Stilp, Cassia Streb, Christine Tavolacci, Jean Thévenet, Ashley Tickle, Melissa Tong, Kerry Tribe, Lawson White, Darryl Williams, Anna Wittenberg, and Manoela Wunder.

Special thanks to Michael Webster.

Performance Notes

Performers should bear in mind that for a cricket, every utterance is "one"–each chirp is complete, not felt as part of a phrase. Soloists should take care to deliver repeated notes with the same technique; bowing in the same direction where practical, for example. In some of the sections, for instance numbers *2* and *8*, there are two players chirping alike but at different dynamics. What is being represented here is a difference in distance from an imaginary microphone rather than a difference in intensity. Mood and technique vary no more between crickets than between chirps.

By and large, conventional expressive musical sounds are to be avoided. Violins and flutes should play *senza vibrato* except when explicitly instructed.

In some vignettes a single soloist may chirp in the foreground while the distant multitude of his fellows is represented by a cluster in the violins. Bearing that in mind, care can be taken to be sure that the tone of that portion of the cluster is appropriate. When the accompanying cluster includes pitches far from that of the soloists, these are likely produced by other insects: in those cases some difference in tone may be welcome.

In the recordings that are the basis of this work sections are generally cross-faded from one to the next. Bear this in mind when transitioning between sections: long initial *crescendi* should be *da niente*, technique permitting, and final *decrescendi* likewise. These may also be extended if convenient.

One sound that should be scrupulously avoided is the sound of strings tuning within a section. If it is absolutely necessary to adjust, try to do so between notes, or simply forge ahead in a kind of *ad hoc* cluster; either is preferable to hearing a pitch sliding.

When orchestra bell keys are rasped by threaded rods or rhythm sticks they should be held pinched on or resting on their nodes so that they ring as well as possible. When the shakers and maracas are shaken or brushed, or the ride cymbal spun, care should be taken to minimize any impression of pulsation: these are meant to be constant environmental noises.

Finally, as regards rhythm, there are few coincidences between lines, and little significance to these. Beyond that, the rhythmic relationships, excepting the percussion duet, are not precious–take care, even when the counting is thorny, to remain, if not serene, let's say matter-of-fact.

Michael Webster
Los Angeles, 2013

Acknowledgements

Thanks to Cecilia Alemani, Crystal Alforque, Brody Albert, Edvard Baratyan, Alessandra Barrett, Jordan Benke, Lionel Bovier, Grace Bowen, Rod Bradley, Ezra Buchla, Paul Calderon, Daniel Cantagallo, Renata Catambas, Benny Chan, Caroline Chin, Tom Chiu, Eric KM Clark, Matthew Cook, Joe Day, Nina Hachigian Day, Keats Diffenbach, Corey Fogel, Pala Garcia, Carissa Gibson, Benjamin Goldenstein, Blanca Gonzalez, Lisa Grzanka, Jessica Han, Orin Hildestad, James Honaker, Robert Johnstone, Christoph Keller, Cindy Kendall, Lauri Firstenberg, Stina Haroldsdottir, Thomai Hatsios, Sarah Hodges, Amanda Hunt, Maria Im, Heather Lockie, Gregory Maldonado, Emanouil Manolov, Richard Massey, Adriana Molello, Aram Moshayedi, Esther Noh, Dimitry Olevsky, Courtney Orlando, Ben Phelps, Monique Prieto, Jean C. Roché, Danielle Roderick, Heber Rodriguez, Albert Romero, Jessica Schmitz, Matthew Schum, Chihiro Shibayama, Stephanie Smith, Alex Sramek, Andy Stanojevich, Mary Jo Stilp, Cassia Streb, Christine Tavolacci, Jean Thévenet, Ashley Tickle, Melissa Tong, Kerry Tribe, Lawson White, Darryl Williams, Anna Wittenberg, and Manoela Wunder.

Special thanks to Michael Webster.

Crickets was first performed on January 28, 2012
during The Ball of Artists, the closing event
of the Pacific Standard Time Public Art and Performance Festival
at Greystone Mansion & Park, Beverly Hills
with the composer conducting